A CASE FOR ONTOLOPHEMES

Icosikaihexagon and Icosihenagon

English's alphabet as a sacred geometrical ontology of graphemes

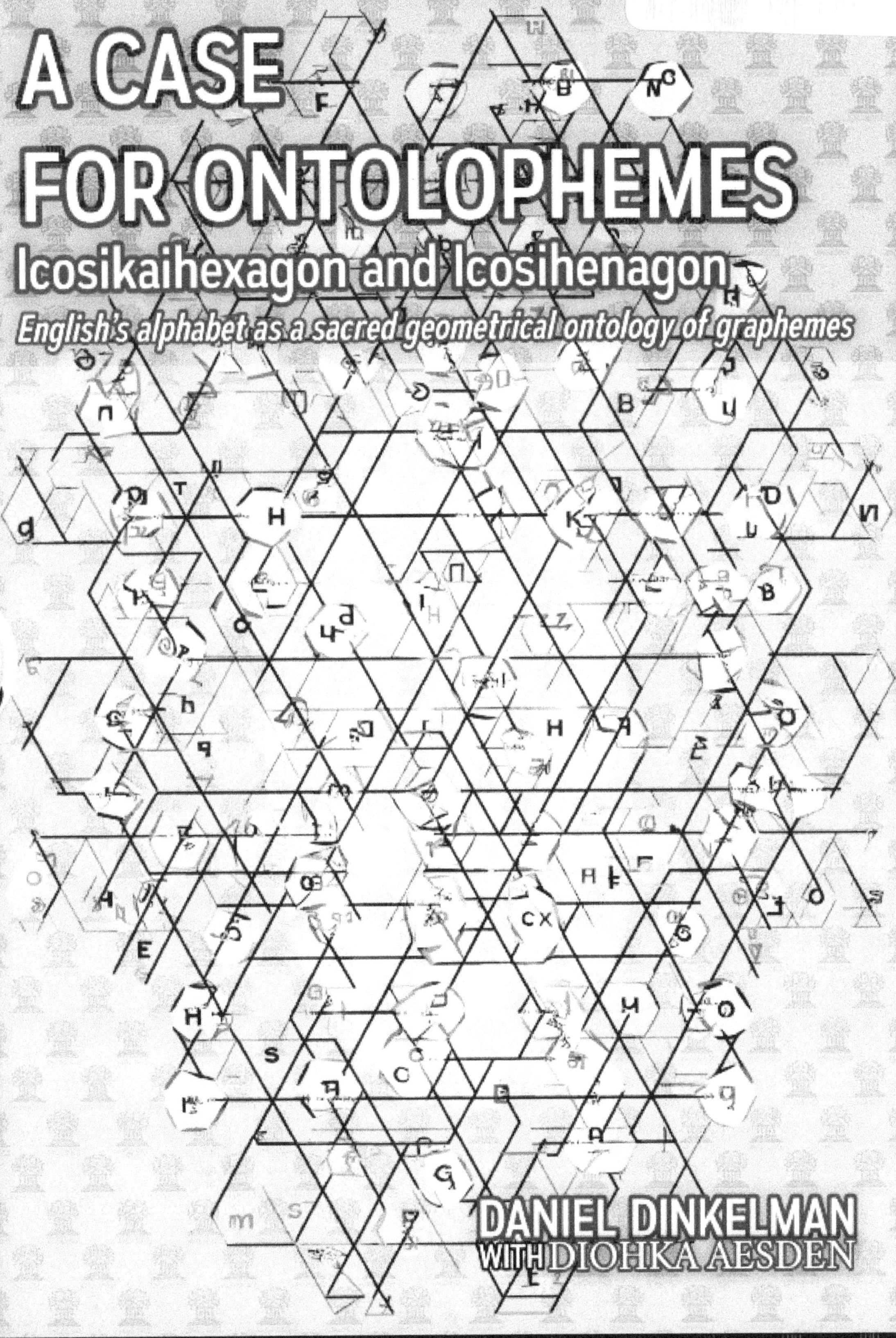

DANIEL DINKELMAN
with DIOHKA AESDEN

Linguistics Series
A Case for Ontolophemes
Icosikaihexagon and Icosihenagon
English's Alphabet as a Sacred Geometrical Ontology of Graphemes

Authors: Daniel Dinkelman, Diohka Aesden
Publisher: Cineris Multifacet
Publication Date: 2025
ISBN: 979-8-89760-036-6

Copyright © 2025 by Cineris Multifacet
All rights reserved. No part of this publication may be reproduced, stored in a retrieval system, or transmitted in any form or by any means, electronic, mechanical, photocopying, recording, or otherwise, without the prior permission of the publisher.

For inquiries and permissions, please contact:
Cineris Multifacet
cinerismultifacet@gmail.com

Design and Typesetting:
Cineris Multifacet

Cover Design:
Cineris Multifacet

Disclaimer: The views and opinions expressed in this book are solely those of the author and do not necessarily mirror the official policy or position of the publisher. The publisher is not responsible for any errors or omissions in the content.

Written in Egypt

First Edition: 2025

ISBN-13: 979-8-89760-036-6

19   54   95

A CASE FOR ONTOLOPHEMES
Icosikaihexagon and Icosihenagon
English's Alphabet as a Sacred Geometrical Ontology of Graphemes

DANIEL DINKELMAN
DIOHKA AESDEN

ORIGINAL BOOKS IN THIS SERIES

1. Computational Linguistics and Artificial Intelligence
2. Sociolinguistics in the Digital Era
3. Historical Linguistics and Language Evolution
4. Psycholinguistics and Neurolinguistics
5. Forensic Linguistics
6. Applied Linguistics in Professional Contexts
7. Philosophical Linguistics and Semiotics
8. Language and Culture
9. Language Technology and Innovation
10. Ethnolinguistics and Linguistic Anthropology
11. Esoteric Linguistics and Communication (with Diohka Aesden)

T o C

OPENING 1

    I. Introduction 5

    1. Statement of Purpose 6

    2. Scope and Significance 12

    3. Methodology 18

II. Foundational Concepts 27

    A. Alphabets as Ontologies 28

    B. The Coined Term: "Ontolopheme" 39

    C. Sacred Geometry and the Alphabet 52

III. Genealogy of the English Alphabet 69

    A. From Proto-Sinaitic to Phoenician 70

    B. Greek Adaptation 80

    C. Latin and the Emergence of 26 Letters 91

IV. The 21 Fundamental Objects (Icosihenagon) 103

    A. Master List of Core Ontic Units 103

V. The 26 Visible Letters (Icosikaihexagon) 131

    A. Practical Exoteric Dimension 132

    B. Case Studies 149

VI. Esoteric and Spiritual Dimensions 159
A. Spelling as "Spellcraft" 160
B. Persistence of "Fundamental Objects" in the Physical World ... 172

VII. Applications and Future Directions 185
A. Re-enchanting Modern Literacy 186
B. Conlang Design and "Ontic Alphabets" 197
C. Digital Age and AI "Spelling" 206

VIII. Conclusion 217

APPENDICES 231
Appendix A: Tables of Letters and Their Phonemes 232
Appendix B: Visual Charts 238
Appendix C: Esoteric and Historical Reference Works 240

REFERENCES 245

OPENING

    This book originally sprang out of an off-the-cuff discussion Diohka and I were having that I had no expectation would evolve into an entire exploration, but it seems there was more here than we at first thought. We've since decided to flesh out the rest of this idea in order to share it with both the linguistic and esoteric community. Herein lies the proposition and coining of the term "ontolophemes" which we hope will become a useful handle for a very observable phenomenon within linguistics, esoteric philosophy, and phenomenology in general.

    Any feedback on this publication or its themes discussed can be left as a comment or review on the marketplace where the book was found. Additionally there is an email address in the opening verso where inquiries can be sent. We thank you so much for perusing this topic of our scholarship and we wish you the best in your study and research in general.

    To the furtherance of all consciousness,

Daniel Dinkelman

I. INTRODUCTION

1. Statement of Purpose

Alphabets have long been treated as convenient repositories for representing the sounds of spoken language, with discussions often centering on phonetic accuracy and orthographic conventions (Sampson, 1985). Yet a deeper lens reveals that an alphabet can function as more than a mere phonetic scaffolding. It can encapsulate an entire worldview, embodying the foundational concepts, tangible objects, or sacred forces that shaped a people's cosmology. The notion of alphabets as **ontologies** – structured inventories of fundamental realities – offers a perspective that unites linguistic history, cognitive anthropology, and spiritual inquiry. Indeed, in many ancient cultures, letters served not only to record speech but also to mirror and engage with the environment, interlacing nature, myth, and practical communication into a cohesive symbolic system (Gelb, 1952).

In the present work, we adopt the term **ontolophemes** to foreground this dimension of writing systems. By "ontolophemes," we refer to letters viewed explicitly as **ontic units**, each representing an idea, object, or domain integral to a cultural worldview. With this conceptual framework, the English alphabet ceases to appear as a purely exoteric set of 26 letters; instead, it stands revealed as a **sacred geometrical ontology** – an icosikaihexagon in its contemporary shape, but rooted in an older icosihenagon of fundamental meanings from the Semitic scripts that preceded it (Daniels & Bright, 1996). Through these pages, the tension between the 26-sided "polygon" we employ daily and the 21-sided "proto-ontology" underlying it will serve as a guiding motif, illuminating how even the most mundane letters carry vestiges of ancient objects and cosmic symbols.

Icosikaihexagon and Icosihenagon

Alphabets as Ontologies

The idea that alphabets function as ontologies emerges from a realization that many writing systems, especially those of antiquity, originated in pictographic or ideographic forms. Proto-Sinaitic letters, for instance, often depicted key items from pastoral or agrarian life – oxen, houses, fish, and so forth – thus providing scribes and readers with a microcosm of their broader environment (DeFrancis, 1989). While the shapes of letters eventually underwent abstraction in Phoenician and Greek adaptations, the *names* of these letters frequently preserved their ancient associations. Thus, "Aleph" (𐤀) conveyed the notion of an "ox," "Beth" (𐤁) evoked a "house," and "Gimel" (𐤂) hinted at a "camel." Over time, these referents became more symbolic and less visually explicit, yet the conceptual core persisted, bridging daily life and cosmic patterns.

Such a phenomenon exemplifies how alphabets can be understood not just as **phoneme inventories** but as **inventories of being**, a term that resonates with the ontological approach. If an alphabet enumerates the "essences" its parent culture deemed vital for representation, each grapheme becomes a window into that society's worldview – an *ontolopheme*, inseparable from the environment, economy, and spiritual inclinations of its users. The present treatise harnesses this dual perspective: on one side, the exoteric reality that we commonly teach in literacy programs, and on the other, the esoteric dimension where letters preserve or imply an older metaphysical significance.

The Icosikaihexagon of Modern English

When viewed superficially, modern English orthography enshrines a convenient set of 26 letters (A through Z). Although certain letters, such as **C**, **Q**, or **X**, present phonetic inconsistencies, the overall system remains functional enough to capture standard English usage, despite extensive

A Case for Ontolophemes

irregularities in spelling (Crystal, 2003). From a strictly functional standpoint, these 26 graphemes operate as the discrete building blocks for written communication, much like 26 edges in a closed geometric figure. One could imagine each letter as a side of an **icosikaihexagon** – a polygon with 26 sides – where each side is equally visible and seemingly independent. Language learners, linguists, and everyday writers typically concern themselves with how these units map onto phonemes or how they blend in morphological composition. The esoteric or conceptual dimension seldom surfaces in standard orthographic discourse.

Beyond orthography, the icosikaihexagonal form also symbolizes the proliferation that has occurred through historical layering. English inherited the Roman alphabet, which, in turn, emerged from Etruscan and Greek precedents. In that lineage, certain letters were split or duplicated to accommodate evolving phonemic distinctions: for instance, the way Latin **V** eventually branched into **U**, **V**, and **W** to represent both vowel and consonant sounds (Haarmann, 1990). Meanwhile, **I** and **J** separated in medieval Latin contexts to mark distinctions between the vowel /i/ and the consonant /dʒ/. Thus, the final count of 26 letters in English results from processes of differentiation and adaptation rather than an original blueprint designed around 26 distinct conceptual objects.

The Icosihenagon of Ancient Roots

When one delves beneath these expansions, a more tightly knit set of roughly 21 "fundamental objects" emerges from the Phoenician script, which itself drew from Proto-Sinaitic or Proto-Canaanite sources (Sass, 1988). The Phoenician script, containing 22 letters, famously names each glyph after an everyday or culturally significant item: **Ox** (Aleph), **House** (Beth), **Camel** (Gimel), **Door** (Daleth), **Fish** (Nun), **Water** (Mem), and so on. After accounting for duplications – instances where a single Phoenician letter gave rise to multiple Latin letters (as with **Yod** engendering both **I** and

J, or **Waw** splitting into **U**, **V**, **W**, and **Y**) – one discovers an underlying ontology of about 21 unique concepts. Hence arises the metaphor of the **icosihenagon**, a 21-sided polygon that hints at this streamlined, conceptual skeleton.

Each side in this "polygon" could be seen as an ancient ontolopheme symbolizing a key facet of Bronze Age Levantine life, from agrarian references like the **Ox** (representing sustenance and power) to domestic images such as the **House** or **Door** (signifying shelter or thresholds). This set of objects constituted a cultural cosmos in miniature. For instance, **Beth** not only denoted a dwelling but connoted broader notions of hearth, family, and communal identity (Cross, 1980). The potency of such associations underscored the letter's capacity to function as more than a phonetic sign; it was an emblem of fundamental being in the daily experience of its users.

The Tension Between 26 and 21

Consequently, there is a nuanced tension at play: while contemporary English usage rests comfortably on 26 letters, the "proto-ontology" beneath them, shaped centuries or millennia earlier, embodies only about 21 distinct symbolic units. This discrepancy reminds us that writing systems evolve through historical layering. Superficially, the system we employ today (the icosikaihexagon) appears stable, but genealogically it is an expanded outgrowth of more focused conceptual roots (the icosihenagon). Recognizing this schism can reorient how we discuss literacy, cultural transmission, and the esoteric dimension of writing.

Furthermore, from the standpoint of **sacred geometry**, these two polygons hint at different approaches to comprehending language. The 26-sided figure of modern usage has an exoteric clarity – every letter stands on its own, making no direct reference to an older worldview. Meanwhile, the 21-sided figure arises from a simpler cosmic grammar, where each letter traces back to a defining object in a pastoral or agricultural setting. This older shape, while not literally recognized in classroom alphabets, suggests that beneath the expansions, duplications, and orthographic shifts, there resides a venerable substrate of conceptual "stones" upon which the edifice of modern literacy was constructed (Daniels & Bright, 1996).

Toward a Re-enchantment of the Alphabet

By proposing the term *ontolophemes*, we aim to bridge the gap between these forms: the visible 26 letters and their hidden 21 conceptual ancestors. Just as a cartouche in ancient Egypt visually encompassed the royal name while symbolically alluding to divine protection, an English sentence – though spelled via 26 distinct letters – can be read as the sum of intangible, archaic forces. Each grapheme, in theory, retains a vestigial imprint of an older ontology tied to the land, to livestock, to human invention, and even to spiritual or cosmic themes (Haarmann, 1990).

Reclaiming this perspective does not require abandoning modern linguistics; indeed, the methodical classification of phonemes, graphemes, and morphological patterns remains invaluable. Rather, it calls on us to acknowledge the layered nature of scripts. Such an acknowledgment can enrich fields as diverse as semiotics, narrative theory, and cultural anthropology, showing how **spelling** is not merely the mechanical arrangement of letters but a potential act of conjuring ancient images and relations.

Concluding Overview of the Introduction

In sum, this introduction contends that the English alphabet, often viewed as a neutral expository tool, can be appreciated as a **sacred geometrical ontology** underpinned by archaic concepts. The exoteric shape of 26 letters – an icosikaihexagon – coexists with an esoteric framework of 21 ontic units – an icosihenagon. Throughout the chapters that follow, we will unravel how these layers emerged historically, were maintained or obscured through cultural transitions, and might be reactivated in contemporary linguistic discourse. Drawing on evidence from comparative script studies (Gelb, 1952; Daniels & Bright, 1996), anthropological linguistics (Crystal, 2003; DeFrancis, 1989), and esoteric interpretations of writing (Haarmann, 1990), we intend to offer a multidimensional view that unites scholarship, introspection, and the living environment into a cohesive argument for alphabets as ontological systems. Such an argument highlights how the act of "spelling" extends beyond phonetic notation, potentially bridging the present with the timeless realms of conceptual archetypes.

2. Scope and Significance

Understanding the scope and significance of an alphabet as a sacred geometrical ontology – where letters function as **ontolophemes** – transcends typical considerations of orthography and spelling. This endeavor re-enchants our view of written language, bridging the apparent gap between its mundane, day-to-day usage and the potent mythic or symbolic origins that shaped it over millennia (Sampson, 1985). Although modern English script might appear purely functional, closer inspection discloses how this 26-letter array is but the latest evolution of an intricate textual lineage reaching back to Phoenician, Proto-Sinaitic, and even earlier symbolic forms (Daniels & Bright, 1996). Through such retrospective analysis, we encounter the compelling reality that alphabets can serve not just as mechanical mappings of phonemes but as storied inventories of fundamental cultural and cosmological ideas.

Re-enchanting Our Understanding of Written Language

Ancient societies across the globe often viewed the written word as imbued with spiritual or magical potency. Egyptian hieroglyphs, for instance, functioned both as vehicles of recorded language and as hieratic symbols of cosmic truths, with certain images (e.g., the falcon representing Horus) implicating divine presences in everyday texts (Manley, 2012). Within the context of Semitic scripts, this spiritual gravitas manifested differently, yet carried parallel resonances. The earliest alphabetical systems – commonly traced to Proto-Sinaitic or Proto-Canaanite – featured pictographic shapes linked to tangible realities: an ox head for **Aleph**, a house plan for **Beth**, or water waves for **Mem** (Sass, 1988). By encoding everyday objects and experiences into a compact repertoire of symbols, these systems materialized an active spiritual worldview, one where each glyph anchored a cultural pillar.

Icosikaihexagon and Icosihenagon

In shifting perspective from a purely **functional** to a more **cosmological** vantage, we may begin to see how modern alphabets hold vestiges of this older, mythic resonance (Sampson, 1985). The notion of "re-enchantment" involves recognizing that even the most routine act of writing an email or drafting a short text entails deploying a set of signs whose genealogical roots once sustained a community's sense of the sacred. These letters are not arbitrary signs but rather the residues of dynamic cultural processes that conjoined practical survival, linguistic expression, and ritual life. Although centuries of phonetic abstraction have distanced our day-to-day writing from its animistic or spiritual forebears, glimpses of the original significance persist in letter names, shapes, and symbolic associations (DeFrancis, 1989).

Consider, for instance, **Aleph** (𐤀), conventionally associated with an "ox." The ox was central to agrarian or pastoral economies in the Eastern Mediterranean, signifying strength, utility, and wealth (Cross, 1980). In modern English, "A" no longer conjures a bovine image or any sense of fertility and labor, but historically, this letter derived from a glyph representing an ox's head. When we contemplate that metamorphosis, we glimpse a radical shift from pictographic meaning to phonetic function – yet that older significance does not vanish so much as lie dormant, ready to be rediscovered by those intrigued by the archaic, symbolic dimension of script (Gelb, 1952).

Re-enchantment, then, does not insist we revert to a pre-scientific worldview. Instead, it invites us to see that linguistic signs carry layered histories. For anthropologists, semioticians, and historically minded linguists, graphemes function as doorways to ancient conceptual ecologies, confirming that the alphabet is not solely a mundane script but a repository of communal memory (Haarmann, 1990). Those memories may include gestures toward divinities, totemic animals, or social institutions (houses, fences, doors) that shaped early societies. In acknowledging this, we reconcile the practical requirements of modern language usage with the mythic origins of alphabetical writing.

Bridging Mundane Usage and Mythic Origins

The perceived tension between the utilitarian function of an alphabet and the sacred or esoteric connotations of its glyphs emerges directly from diachronic change – linguistic evolution over extended periods (Crystal, 2003). Borrowings, adaptations, and phonological shifts accumulate layer upon layer of transformation, such that contemporary readers rarely recognize the earlier function of their alphabetic letters. This results in an alphabet that appears "neutral," while still retaining skeletal outlines that, in earlier epochs, comprised a sacred order. In bridging mundane usage and mythic roots, one must examine how writing systems originated, adapted, and diversified as they passed from one culture to another.

Proto-Sinaitic inscriptions, discovered in regions like Serabit el-Khadim (in the Sinai Peninsula), demonstrate a transitional phase between Egyptian hieroglyphic or hieratic scripts and the emergent Semitic alphabets (Sass, 1988). Although archaeologists and epigraphers debate the exact timeline and modes of cultural exchange, consensus holds that certain workers or scribes familiar with Egyptian iconography began reassigning Egyptian signs to represent the consonantal sounds of their own Semitic language. Crucially, these adaptations were not random: many signs corresponded to culturally salient objects, such as cattle for economic sustenance or houses for kinship structures (Cross, 1980). Thus, from the earliest stages, the letters themselves formed an **ontic** landscape – a symbolic map of essential daily realities.

Over generations, Proto-Sinaitic evolved into **Proto-Canaanite**, which later gave rise to **Phoenician**. The Phoenicians, famed maritime traders, transmitted a refined 22-letter system across the Mediterranean, eventually influencing the Greek adoption of these glyphs (Daniels & Bright, 1996).

Greek scribes introduced vowels into an alphabet that was predominantly consonantal, an innovation with profound implications for textual clarity and expressive range (DeFrancis, 1989). Yet even while new letter forms arose – Alpha, Beta, Gamma, Delta – the underlying notion that each glyph once pointed to a fundamental object or concept never entirely vanished. Alpha still harkened back to the ox, albeit indirectly, while Beta gestured to the house, long after Phoenician had reshaped it visually and functionally.

Latin then adapted the Greek alphabet, particularly through Etruscan intermediaries, leading to further expansions. Latin script introduced minor modifications – such as the addition or reintroduction of letters like **G** – aimed at capturing specific phonemic contrasts (Sampson, 1985). Later medieval developments, most notably the splitting of **U** and **V**, as well as **I** and **J**, compounded the complexity, generating the standard 26 letters that modern English speakers take for granted (Crystal, 2003). Each adaptation retained the functional necessity of representing speech sounds but often obscured the archaic, mythic correlation between letters and material or cosmic objects.

Yet, a genealogical thread remains. It is that invisible chain linking **Aleph** to **Alpha**, then to **A**, or that interlaces **Beth** to **Beta** to **B**. In bridging the mundane usage of present-day orthography to its mythic origin, one must undertake a form of **textual archaeology**: unearthing how each letter – though now an abstract sign – once engaged with a tangible reality. Through the concept of **ontolophemes**, we awaken to this earlier mode of significance. Rather than dismissing letters as inert forms, we can conceive of them as vestigial "capsules" of older cultural knowledge, whose references range from pastoral life to proto-cosmological understanding.

From Early Semitic Scripts to Modern English

Tracing the route from **Proto-Sinaitic** to modern English merges the concerns of epigraphy, historical linguistics, and cultural anthropology. Scholars in epigraphy have unearthed tablets, graffiti, and inscriptions showing how letters shifted shape and meaning over centuries (Sass, 1988). Historical linguists document the phonetic changes that prompted script adjustments, while anthropologists contextualize these developments in broader socio-political or religious frameworks.

Phoenician, as a transitional script, represents a linchpin in this narrative. Because Phoenician traders traveled widely, they introduced the concept of a consonantal alphabet to various cultures around the Mediterranean, ultimately influencing the Ionian and Dorian Greeks (Daniels & Bright, 1996). When the Greeks integrated vowels, the writing system gained new clarity, facilitating the proliferation of literature, philosophy, and eventually science.

From there, **Latin** appropriation of the Greek alphabet, aided by Etruscan mediation, laid the foundation for the Western alphabets we know today (Sampson, 1985). By the time this lineage arrived at English, centuries of Celtic, Germanic, Norman, and Romance influences had shaped the language's phonology and orthographic demands. The introduction of printing technology in the late Middle Ages and Renaissance standardized spelling even as the oral dimension continued changing. Ultimately, the English alphabet's emergence as a 26-letter exoteric system concealed the deeper genealogical arc that once manifested an older cosmic or ecological worldview.

Significance for Contemporary Linguistic and Cultural Studies

Recognizing the script's dual nature – mundane on the surface, mythic at its core – provides a **catalyst for interdisciplinary scholarship**. Educators can illuminate the origin of letters in classroom literacy programs, offering students a richer contextual frame that infuses reading and writing with cultural and historical resonance (Haarmann, 1990).

Icosikaihexagon and Icosihenagon

Folklorists and mythographers gain insight into how symbolic objects (ox, house, door, fish) persist in the collective memory through the continuity of script. Conlangers, or constructed language enthusiasts, can draw inspiration from the synergy of ancient symbol and modern function, crafting new alphabets that intentionally embed mythic or ecological references into their glyphs.

Furthermore, bridging the gap between mundane usage and mythic origin underscores the principle that **human communication is rarely neutral** – it is steeped in cultural and historical sediment. Even as we dash off text messages or emails, we unconsciously deploy signs whose lineage traverses centuries of adaptation, conquest, trade, and religious transformation (Crystal, 2003). To adopt an ontological perspective on these letters is to perceive, in everyday typing, a faint echo of temple incantations, pastoral labor, or navigational commerce. In acknowledging that echo, we affirm the significance of harnessing historical awareness to inform present practices, thereby preserving a sense of wonder and depth that can so easily be lost in modern literacy.

3. Methodology

The investigation of alphabets as **sacred geometrical ontologies** requires a methodology that traverses diverse scholarly terrains, intertwining **linguistic history**, **esoteric traditions**, and **sacred geometry**. This threefold approach enables us to illuminate the idea that letters (or **ontolophemes**) are not merely phonetic placeholders, but rather nodes in a vast symbolic network. By showing how each letter evolved through specific cultural, mystical, and geometric lenses, we attempt to substantiate the claim that contemporary scripts, including the modern English alphabet, retain vestiges of older conceptual frameworks (Daniels & Bright, 1996; Gelb, 1952). This section clarifies our methodological blueprint, explaining how we draw from historical linguistics, textual archaeology, comparative symbolism, and geometric analysis to highlight the deeper ontic significance of graphemes.

3.1 A Multi-Disciplinary Framework

3.1.1 Historical Linguistics and Epigraphy

A foundational cornerstone of this research is the **historical–linguistic** examination of scripts, tracing genealogical lineages from early Semitic writing systems through Greek, Latin, and finally to modern English (Sass, 1988). By reviewing epigraphic evidence – namely inscriptions, tablets, and manuscripts – we reconstruct a narrative of how each letter's form and function transformed over centuries (Cross, 1980). This process reveals the diachronic layering that ultimately allowed a 22-letter Phoenician script to expand (through intermediate adaptations) into the 26-letter English repertoire.

- Key Sources:
    - **Proto-Sinaitic artifacts** from the Sinai Peninsula, demonstrating transitional pictographic–alphabetic forms (Sass, 1988).
    - **Phoenician inscriptions** detailing how letter names corresponded to cultural objects (Aleph = "ox," Beth = "house," etc.).
    - **Greek and Latin manuscripts**, which illustrate morphological shifts – such as the insertion of vowel letters in Greek and the duplication of letters in Latin (Sampson, 1985).

Such materials are analyzed with attention to scribal habits, orthographic innovations, and phonetic requirements. By correlating historical usage patterns with morphological changes, we identify how certain letters came to represent distinct phonemes or conceptual references. This genealogical perspective is crucial: it offers a concrete foundation to the claim that behind modern alphabets lie earlier symbolic systems shaped by environment, livelihood, and cosmology (DeFrancis, 1989).

3.1.2 Esoteric Traditions and Symbolic Interpretation

While historical linguistics concentrates on how scripts fulfill communicative functions, **esoteric traditions** emphasize the mystical or symbolic weight that letters carry. Ancient civilizations frequently attributed cosmological, magical, or sacred connotations to their scripts (Manley, 2012). For instance, Egyptian hieroglyphic writing often conflated phonetic use with ritual significance, as seen in the depiction of falcons and other animals aligned with deities. Similarly, Hebrew mysticism (Kabbalah) associates each letter with cosmic energies, numeric values, and hidden frameworks of creation (Haarmann, 1990). Although our primary focus is on Phoenician, Proto-Sinaitic, Greek, and Latin alphabets, these near-parallel developments in Egyptian and

A Case for Ontolophemes

Semitic contexts underscore the broader phenomenon of letters as carriers of intangible power.

In exploring these esoteric dimensions, we rely on:

- **Mythographical analyses** of letter names and shapes, such as the transition from "ox" (Aleph) to "Alpha," and how the original concept may persist as a latent symbol of strength or primal force.

- **Comparative religious studies** that investigate how different cultures used scripts in protective amulets, religious liturgies, or incantations (Sampson, 1985).

- **Anthropological perspectives** on how preliterate societies assigned spiritual or animistic properties to visual symbols, setting precedents for later alphabets.

Such materials feed into an interpretative framework: letters, beyond phonemes, can act as gateways to conceptual or mythic realms. In the context of the English alphabet, even though the immediate association with cosmic or agrarian objects has largely faded, these deeper resonances can be excavated through historical and cultural cross-analysis (Crystal, 2003).

3.1.3 Sacred Geometry and Structural Analysis

A key addition to our methodology lies in **sacred geometry**, a domain traditionally concerned with geometric patterns believed to reflect divine or natural harmonies. The notion that the **English alphabet** may be visualized as an **icosikaihexagon** (26 sides) and its ancestral substrate as an **icosihenagon** (21 sides) serves a dual function. First, it offers a **metaphorical lens**, enabling us to conceive of alphabets as enclosed wholes with discrete "edges" or "faces" (Gelb, 1952). Second, it highlights the phenomenon of **numerical expansions** in script evolution, wherein a smaller set of essential symbols (the 21 ontic concepts or letter roots) can be multiplied into a larger repertoire as phonemic or functional demands grow.

This sacred-geometric motif does not imply that ancient scribes meticulously drew polygons to plan their alphabets; rather, it underscores the principle of *limited sets of forms* that can comprehensively capture a broader worldview (Haarmann, 1990). By engaging with geometric analogies, we aim to reclaim the sense of wholeness or structural unity that might otherwise be obscured by centuries of incremental change. Ultimately, geometric framing suggests that alphabets can encapsulate cosmic or spiritual order just as well as they map speech onto graphemes.

3.2 Data Collection and Comparative Analysis
3.2.1 Textual Archaeology and Inscriptional Evidence

To operationalize our multi-disciplinary approach, we gather data from a wide array of textual and inscriptional sources. Among these are:

- **Bronze Age and Iron Age inscriptions** discovered in Levantine sites, forming the bedrock of Phoenician script studies (Cross, 1980; Sass, 1988).

- **Greek papyri and stone engravings**, including early examples of written Greek that betray Phoenician influence (Daniels & Bright, 1996).

- **Latin epigraphic monuments** and medieval manuscripts, illustrating the transitional phases that helped shape the modern Roman alphabet.

- **Conjectural reconstructions** in proto-linguistic scholarship, which link specific glyphs (e.g., ⚁ "aleph") to pictographic antecedents (e.g., an ox head).

In analyzing these sources, we implement a **comparative method** that juxtaposes letter shapes, letter names, and documented phonetic values across time (Sampson, 1985). Where textual materials are sparse, we rely on established archaeological or paleographic consensus (e.g., the identification of "Beth" as a schematic house plan). This comparative approach allows us to gauge both the continuity and divergence in how letters have functioned as ontic references.

3.2.2 Linguistic Reconstruction and Etymology of Letter Names

A second critical methodological step involves **linguistic reconstruction**, whereby we trace how letter names morph or adapt as scripts move between cultures. For example, the Hebrew "Aleph" (א) shares a root with Phoenician ⨯ (Aleph) and eventually influenced Greek "Alpha" (A), with the underlying concept of an "ox" (or an "ox head") partially surviving as a lexical memory (Cross, 1980). Similarly, "Beth" (𐤁) signifying a "house" transitions to Greek "Beta" (B), then to Latin "B," even though the everyday user of English rarely envisions four walls and a roof when writing the letter B. By scrutinizing these name changes, we shine light on how cultural-linguistic transmissions gradually abstract out the original referent (DeFrancis, 1989).

Where possible, we correlate these transformations with evidence for how each object – ox, house, fish, water – figured in the society's economic, religious, or ecological life. Hence, the method does not stop at philological detail but extends into cultural anthropology, mapping how references to livestock, shelters, or aquatic resources reflect broader lifeways. This multi-tier analysis clarifies that the morphological shift from pictographic to alphabetic representation is not a severance but a re-layering of older signification (Sass, 1988).

3.2.3 Symbolic Hermeneutics and Esoteric Exegesis

Beyond philological reconstruction, we deploy **symbolic hermeneutics**, an interpretive strategy that reads letters as carriers of symbolic weight. Drawing on hermeneutic anthropology (Clifford, 1986) and comparative religion, we investigate how objects like "Ox" or "Tooth" or "Mark/Cross" possessed not only practical meanings in daily life (e.g., a real ox for plowing) but also metaphysical resonance (e.g., a symbol of fertility, strength, or boundary). Such interpretations may be gleaned from mythic narratives, liturgical texts, or later commentarial traditions that preserved glimpses of the archaic significance behind each letter (Haarmann, 1990).

This hermeneutic dimension ensures that letters are approached not just as linear containers of phonemes but as "ontolophemes," signifying entire conceptual spheres. For instance, one might explore how the letter **Taw** (ת or ✝), originally meaning "mark" or "cross," evolved into a symbol of boundary or identity marking, and eventually took on theological connotations in certain Judaic or Christian contexts. By systematically pairing textual data with symbolic exegesis, the argument for alphabets as ontological frameworks becomes more robust.

3.3 The Newly Coined Concept: Ontolophemes

Central to this methodological lattice is the introduction of **ontolophemes** – a newly minted term to describe letters specifically regarded as **ontic units**. While linguistics traditionally distinguishes graphemes, phonemes, and morphemes, we propose that an ontolopheme diverges by emphasizing a letter's reference to an object or concept that transcends phonetic function. In other words, an ontolopheme is:

"A grapheme whose visual shape, historical lineage, or culturally recognized meaning directly encodes a fundamental concept (e.g., 'ox,' 'house,' 'water'), rather than serving solely as a placeholder for a phoneme."

We posit that each letter within the older Phoenician or Proto-Sinaitic scripts can be understood as an ontolopheme because it was anchored in a real or mythic object from that society's environment or worldview (Sass, 1988). As the script journeyed through Greek, Latin, and eventually English contexts, these letters retained their shapes to varying degrees but were gradually divested of overt conceptual references. The methodology behind **ontolophemes** thus demands an integrated reading of script genealogies, interpretive traditions, and environmental or social contexts, bridging philology and symbolic analysis into a single interpretive framework.

From a methodological stance, acknowledging the existence of ontolophemes enriches the conversation about how writing systems operate at a deeper cultural register. It challenges the default assumption that alphabets are purely phonological tools, suggesting instead that they are also signatories of a collective intellectual and spiritual heritage. This approach aligns with scholarship on **phonosemantic** and **cognitive** aspects of writing, which notes that certain shapes or letter names carry emotive or associative power (Haarmann, 1990). The concept of ontolophemes thus crystallizes these observations, offering a fresh term that can facilitate more nuanced discourse, whether among linguists, historians, or conlang enthusiasts.

3.4 Synthesizing the Approaches

Finally, each of these strands – historical-linguistic reconstruction, esoteric inquiry, and sacred geometry – converges in a **synthesized analysis** that frames the English alphabet both as a **26-sided polygon** (*icosikaihexagon*) and as

Icosikaihexagon and Icosihenagon

an underlying **21-sided conceptual set** (*icosihenagon*). The steps can be summarized as follows:

1. Genealogical Mapping
    - We chart how each modern letter traces its lineage back to a smaller repertoire of Phoenician signs, accounting for phonetic shifts and letter duplications.

2. Symbolic Correlation
    - We revisit the ancient referents (ox, house, door, etc.) that once animated those letters, exploring how each referent corresponded to cultural or mythic significance in early Semitic societies.

3. Geometric and Ontological Interpretation
    - We employ the **icosikaihexagon** as a visual metaphor for English's modern letter inventory and the **icosihenagon** to symbolize the more compact set of archaic ontic referents.
    - This dual framework highlights how expansions and duplications (e.g., the multiple forks of "Waw" into U, V, W, Y) obscure the fact that many letters share a common conceptual root.

By interlacing these interpretive lines, we situate letters within a broad cultural and spiritual cosmos. The methodology thereby underscores that alphabets are not merely mechanical orthographic systems but living records of historical encounters between meaning, environment, and expression (Crystal, 2003). In the following sections, this multi-pronged method will guide our exploration of how everyday written language, seemingly mundane, can reawaken connections to the ancient objects and concepts that once defined entire civilizations.

II. FOUNDATIONAL CONCEPTS

A. Alphabets as Ontologies
1. Defining "Ontology" in Linguistics

In common parlance, the term *ontology* evokes philosophical discussions of being and existence – how entities are classified, what categories they belong to, and what interrelations define them (Smith, 2003). Traditionally, when linguists discuss alphabets, the conversation revolves around **phonemes** and **graphemes** – correspondences designed to represent speech sounds in written form (Sampson, 1985). Mainstream linguistic scholarship largely regards alphabets as **phonetic devices** – codes mapping the sounds of a language onto a visual symbol system. From this perspective, a letter is an abstract unit that, ideally, corresponds to one or more phonemes, with orthographic inconsistencies arising from historical developments rather than design (Crystal, 2003).

However, an alternative view foregrounds the idea that alphabets can serve not merely as mechanical representations of speech but as **ontological frameworks**, each grapheme encoding a profound connection to real-world objects, forces, or concepts. This approach diverges significantly from orthodox linguistic models, positioning graphemes as **ontic units** (or *ontolophemes*) – symbols that once encapsulated entire conceptual domains, whether agrarian (oxen, houses), environmental (water, fish), or cosmic (celestial bodies, gods). In essence, each letter might be an "index" for aspects of a community's worldview, bridging the quotidian and the metaphysical (Haarmann, 1990).

Mainstream Linguistic Views: Phonetics as the Core

Within the mainstream linguistic tradition, alphabets are the culmination of a historical process in which pictographic or logographic systems (such as Egyptian hieroglyphs) gradually shed semantic and iconic components. Over time, they converged on forms that represent discrete phonemes or syllables (DeFrancis, 1989). Thus, in the standard narrative, the emergence of the Phoenician alphabet marks a milestone in human literacy: a major leap that gave societies a streamlined system to map the spoken word onto script. Scholars often emphasize the efficiency of this system, especially when contrasted with character-based scripts, such as Chinese, or logographic syllabaries, like those in Mesopotamia (Justeson & Stephens, 1994).

A particularly influential perspective comes from Saussurean linguistics, wherein speech is considered the **primary** system and writing merely a **secondary** representation (Saussure, 1916/1974). In this framework, graphemes exist mainly to mirror phonemes, and it is the spoken linguistic form that holds primacy in language studies. Following this logic, an "ideal" orthography would yield a one-to-one correspondence between letters and sounds, thus minimizing irregularities and ambiguities (Sampson, 1985).

When viewed through such a lens, **letters** are stripped of much of their cultural or symbolic baggage: they become placeholders for bits of phonetic information. The typical constraints and problematics revolve around how accurately these letters capture spoken nuances (e.g., how to represent diphthongs, nasal vowels, or consonant clusters). Consequently, mainstream discussions often focus on:

- **Orthographic standardization** (e.g., in modern English, the many irregularities that arise from historical spelling conventions).

- **Reform proposals** (e.g., the push for phonetic spelling championed by figures like George Bernard Shaw).

- **Comparative script efficiency** (e.g., how quickly a child can learn a largely phonetic script versus a logographic script).

A Case for Ontolophemes

This is the dominant orientation, one that has indisputably advanced our understanding of how reading, writing, and language acquisition function. Yet it underemphasizes, or in many cases ignores, the historical fact that scripts often began as **symbolic** or **iconic** representations of tangible realities (Gelb, 1952). When a letter was first devised in a Bronze Age community, it might have been a stylized image connoting a meaningful aspect of everyday life. As centuries pass, such iconic references typically fade under layers of abstraction.

The Esoteric Idea: Graphemes as Encoded Objects or Forces

By contrast, the **esoteric** view suggests that letters carry vestigial or concealed symbolic weight, echoing older cosmological or cultural frameworks (Haarmann, 1990). In this approach, the letter is not merely a vessel for a phoneme, but rather a seed that once sprouted from a cultural environment and thus can be interpreted as carrying an entire symbolic or mythic domain. Many esoteric traditions, from Kabbalistic explorations of the Hebrew alphabet to Renaissance occult interpretations of Latin and Greek letters, underscore the notion that each grapheme *embodies* an aspect of reality – whether an ox, a fish, a cross, or a doorway into deeper existential truths (Idel, 1988; Manley, 2012).

The esoteric model gains credibility when we examine the earliest phases of alphabetic writing. For instance, Proto-Sinaitic inscriptions often show recognizable pictorial elements: an ox's head for Aleph, waves for Mem, a triangular doorway for Daleth, and so forth (Sass, 1988). Although these shapes quickly lose clarity as they pass through Phoenician and Greek stylization, the letter names typically preserve the original referent for many generations (DeFrancis, 1989). "Aleph" remains associated with an ox, "Beth" with a house, and "Nun" with a fish, even when the written forms themselves become abstract lines or curves.

Moreover, a distinct feature of esoteric linguistics lies in its **cosmological** dimension. Here, alphabets are seen as microcosms reflecting macrocosmic principles. Hebrew mysticism often views the 22 letters as embodying the creative energies that shaped the cosmos, each letter acting like a blueprint for a strand of existence (Halevi, 1987). While not all scripts receive equally robust mystical elaborations, the underlying insight is that writing is never purely random or mechanistic – it is shaped by the cultural imagination and invests signs with layered significance.

Hence, contrasting these two views – **mainstream phonetics** vs. **esoteric ontology** – sets the stage for a nuanced investigation: alphabets may indeed be essential tools for representing speech, yet they also carry embedded references to conceptual "nodes" that earlier cultures deemed fundamental. Recognizing this duality expands our understanding of how letters function in society, bridging the gap between day-to-day literacy and deeper mythic or spiritual usage (Crystal, 2003).

2. Historical Precedents

If alphabets (and writing systems more generally) can encode such ontic or conceptual material, one would expect to see evidence of this dynamic across different civilizations and script types. Indeed, historical precedents abound, illustrating how writing systems often originated in real-world objects, creatures, or beliefs that were central to the society that created them. While many of these systems eventually evolved into more abstract phonetic forms, the **initial impetus** for a grapheme typically involved a reference to something tangible or revered.

2.1 Egyptian Hieroglyphs

Egyptian hieroglyphs stand out as one of the most richly documented ancient scripts, blending phonetic, ideographic, and symbolic dimensions (Manley, 2012). The term

A Case for Ontolophemes

"hieroglyph" itself derives from Greek for "sacred carving," highlighting the ritual or ceremonial context in which Egyptians employed these signs (Allen, 2014). Hieroglyphs are diverse: some represent entire words, some function as phonetic components, and others as determinatives indicating semantic fields. Yet, crucially, many glyphs directly depict real-world objects or beings:

1. **The "Horus falcon"**: Often seen perched on or near a cartouche, symbolizing kingship and the god Horus. Although it serves multiple linguistic functions – sometimes purely as a determinative for "falcon" or "god" – its visual depiction references an actual bird integral to Egyptian culture, reflecting predator symbolism and divine kingship.

2. **The ankh** ⟨☥⟩: Commonly interpreted as the hieroglyph meaning "life." Despite later being used in stylized contexts, the ankh remains a powerful cultural icon, connoting divine vitality, fertility, and immortality (Manley, 2012).

3. **Everyday objects**: Reed leaves, water waves, bread loaves, and so forth. Each sign might function phonetically, but it also resonates with the crucial environmental or societal roles those objects played along the Nile.

These hieroglyphs illustrate how a script can serve double-duty: *practically*, as a means of communication and *symbolically*, as a cosmic map of the world's essential elements. In essence, they are "ontic seeds" reflecting an Egyptian worldview, replete with references to religion, nature, and monarchy (Haarmann, 1990).

2.2 Sumerian Cuneiform

One of the oldest known writing systems, **Sumerian cuneiform**, provides another illustration of how characters initially grew out of pictographic references to physical objects or concepts. Early Sumerian writing involved clay tablets impressed with wedge-shaped styluses, producing images that schematically represented tangible realities: grain ears, bowls, livestock, and so on (Cooper, 1996). As with Egyptian hieroglyphs, these images gradually underwent standardization, becoming simpler and more abstract in form. Nonetheless, the lexical roots behind many signs remained anchored in the environment and economy of Mesopotamia:

1. **Agricultural symbols**: Representations of a sheaf of grain or a plowed field mirrored a civilization strongly dependent on irrigation-based farming (Kramer, 1963). Over time, these pictographs became linear, wedge-like forms, but their semantics lingered.

2. **Animals and tools**: Sheep, goats, and cattle, as well as hoes, plows, and sickles, were etched onto tablets to track ownership, rations, and tax obligations. Each sign carried immediate practical relevance – how many sheep or bushels of barley a temple had in storage – yet also touched upon the cosmic significance of ensuring abundance and communal prosperity (Postgate, 1994).

As cuneiform advanced into a full-blown syllabary and logography, certain signs began to represent syllables or phonetic clusters rather than their original pictorial meaning. Despite this shift, the underlying impetus – that writing was an instrument to catalog, interpret, and even **shape** the human-environment interface – remained integral. Sumerian cuneiform thus exemplifies how scripts can serve, at their foundation, as ontological inventories of the tangible realm, later morphing into flexible symbolic systems for broader linguistic expression (Black et al., 2006).

2.3 Chinese Characters

Although structurally quite different from alphabetic scripts, **Chinese characters** showcase another prominent instance where real-world items and conceptual fields have been encoded into the shapes of written symbols (DeFrancis, 1984). The Chinese writing system, widely regarded as among the world's oldest continuous literary traditions, includes pictographs, ideographs, and compound characters that merge phonetic and semantic elements. Many of these characters began as direct images of natural or cultural artifacts:

1. **Pictographic origins**: Characters like 日 (rì, "sun") or 月 (yuè, "moon") once bore closer resemblance to their actual shapes. Even today, an imaginative mind can see a rough circle with lines (for "sun") or a stylized crescent (for "moon") in these forms (Hsia, 1992).

2. **Radicals as ontic seeds**: The system of radicals – basic building blocks – often indicates a conceptual domain (e.g., "water," "hand," "heart," "woman," "wood") that influences the overall meaning of a character. Though many radicals no longer look like their original pictorial source, they continue to anchor the lexicon in everyday objects and experiences (DeFrancis, 1984).

Over centuries, calligraphic conventions and dynastic reforms refined these characters, sometimes obscuring earlier pictorial elements. Yet the genealogical record of the script remains richly documented, revealing how fundamental features of the natural world – rivers, trees, heavenly bodies – became the bedrock of a sophisticated literary tradition. This resonates strongly with the notion that writing systems could be read as ontological compendia, each glyph affirming a reality embedded in socio-cultural existence (Haarmann, 1990).

Convergent Patterns in Ancient Scripts

What unifies these three examples – Egyptian hieroglyphs, Sumerian cuneiform, and Chinese characters – is their **shared reliance on everyday realities** to develop an initial roster of symbols. While these scripts later diverged in structure and purpose, all of them illustrate how writing systems can begin as **iconic or semantically loaded** sets of signs. Over time, practical pressures (more fluent writing, desire for broader vocabulary coverage, new linguistic contexts) lead to greater abstraction, reducing the direct pictorial link to the referent object or concept (Gelb, 1952).

In short, each of these major civilizations offers a precedent for how a system of written signs could start out as a reflection of a collective worldview – an "ontology" of objects deemed critical for survival, worship, or cultural identity – and later transition into a more generalized script. Observing these evolutionary pathways provides a macro-template for what happened in the Semitic alphabetic tradition as well, from Proto-Sinaitic and Phoenician to Greek, Latin, and English (Daniels & Bright, 1996). Although alphabets differ in structure from logographic or morphosyllabic systems, they share a comparable historical arc where "real-world items as seeds" gradually yield "abstract symbols for language."

Connecting to the "Ontic Seeds" Concept

The term *ontic seeds* underscores the idea that these fundamental objects or references in a script are **more than** mere placeholders. They are kernels of meaning from which an entire writing system can bloom. If Egyptian or Sumerian scribes recognized that carved signs or wedge marks provided a shorthand for referencing crucial goods, social roles, or divine powers, the same impetus likely informed the creation and naming of Phoenician letters (Cross, 1980). Moreover, the essential logic extends beyond the ancient world: contemporary conlang projects, heavily influenced by Tolkien or modern linguistic theories, sometimes re-introduce the principle of "pictographic impetus," embedding symbolic references into newly minted scripts (Peterson, 2015).

Given these broad historical precedents, we have reason to believe that **alphabets too can be read as ontologies**, even though they have become heavily abstracted and mostly are taught as phonetic systems. This viewpoint reinforces the argument that each letter in the Phoenician and Greek traditions once corresponded to an object or conceptual field relevant to pastoral or urban life – e.g., an "ox" or a "house" for the early Semites, a "camel" or a "fish," all of which had daily and spiritual significance (Sass, 1988). That these older references are no longer recognized by modern English speakers does not negate their genealogical import. The creation of an "A" from an ox head or a "B" from a house blueprint signals that phonetics was only part of the original impetus.

Significance for Understanding Modern Alphabets

Reflecting on these historical precedents broadens our lens when approaching **English orthography**. Commonly, students are taught that letters such as "A" and "B" correspond to certain phonemes (/eɪ/, /b/), and one might rarely proceed beyond those immediate functions. However, a genealogical vantage reveals that these letters anchor deeper strata of cultural history. "A," in a sense, remains a glyph that once stood for an ox head, symbolizing provision, labor, and strength in pastoral societies (Cross, 1980). "B" once connoted a house, pivotal to domestic security and communal identity. Such associations arguably form a layer of **mythic subtext** that persists despite the surface-level transformations across time (DeFrancis, 1989).

By recognizing that **hieroglyphic** systems, **cuneiform** systems, and **Chinese** characters underwent parallel evolutions, we grasp that the "ontic impetus" is not unique to alphabets, nor is it a fleeting curiosity. Rather, it appears consistently across human writing traditions, which seemingly start with references to the tangible environment – cattle, farmland, astral bodies, local fauna – and gradually expand and refine those references into intricate, versatile scripts. In each case, the impetus for writing ties to a deeper existential set of concerns, whether managing resources, venerating deities, or constructing cosmic meaning (Haarmann, 1990).

Reframing alphabets as ontologies thus becomes part of a larger conversation about the **cultural and cognitive roots** of writing. As writing is transferred from one linguistic environment to another – such as Phoenician scripts being adapted by Greek city-states – the original "ontic seeds" might fade or distort. New users might preserve letter shapes but lose track of their semantic heritage, focusing primarily on phonetic utility (Sampson, 1985). Nevertheless, textual archaeology and epigraphic studies allow us to piece together these older layers, reminding us that behind the shapes of letters lie fundamental references to the environment, economy, and spirituality of ancient peoples.

Concluding Thoughts on Foundations

In sum, "alphabets as ontologies" stems from the recognition that:

1. **Mainstream Linguistics** typically treats alphabets in a phonetic capacity, focusing on the one-to-one (or near one-to-one) mapping between letters and sounds.

2. **Esoteric or Symbolic Perspectives** propose that each grapheme can also encode a *fundamental object or force*, thus rendering alphabets as condensed maps of a cultural worldview.

3. **Historical Precedents** in scripts like Egyptian hieroglyphs, Sumerian cuneiform, and Chinese characters illustrate how writing systems often begin with direct references to tangible realities or cosmic phenomena, which they gradually streamline over time.

Accepting the latter viewpoint does not negate the practicality of alphabets as phonetic tools but instead enriches it, implying that present usage resonates with older cultural frameworks. This perspective resonates with the experiences of many ancient scribes who lived in a realm where "writing" and "world" were not neatly separated domains: each sign within a script anchored a particular, vital domain – cattle, shelter, fish, water, star, or deity. Such synergy between language, culture, and environment persists in often-unrecognized ways, offering an alternative vantage for understanding the significance of letters even in modern contexts like English (Manley, 2012).

The next chapters will build on this conceptual framework, shedding light on how the English alphabet in particular evolved from a more **focused set** of objects – arguably around 21 of them – into a **26-letter** arrangement. By correlating the mainstream phonetic lens with the esoteric or ontological approach, we reintroduce readers to the fundamental insight that writing is not a mere code but a total lattice of references to the lived realities of the societies that forged it (Crystal, 2003). A deeper comprehension of these references fosters both historical awareness and a renewed sense of mystery concerning the simple act of "spelling." If an alphabet is indeed an ontology, then each grapheme stands as a silent witness to the union of language, environment, and spirit – a far cry from a trivial marker of sound.

B. The Coined Term: "Ontolopheme"

1. Etymology and Definition

The concept of the **ontolopheme** emerges at the intersection of linguistics, semiotics, and cultural anthropology. Unlike standard descriptive terms such as *phoneme*, *morpheme*, or *grapheme*, the neologism *ontolopheme* recognizes a grapheme's deeper capacity to represent not merely a sound or a writing unit, but an entire conceptual or cosmological domain. This newly coined term foregrounds the belief that certain letters – especially in archaic or semi-pictorial scripts – are best understood as "ontic portals," each symbolically linked to a fundamental concept or object that anchored the worldview of the script's originating community.

1.1 Breaking Down the Term: *Ontos + Lophos + -eme*

In conventional linguistic taxonomy, the suffix *-eme* denotes the smallest meaningful unit in a given linguistic or semiotic category (Crystal, 2003). For instance:

- A **phoneme** is the smallest unit of sound distinguishing meaning in a language (e.g., /p/ vs. /b/ in English).

- A **morpheme** is the smallest unit bearing semantic content (e.g., "cat" or the plural suffix "-s").

- A **grapheme** is the smallest distinctive unit in a writing system (e.g., "a," "b," or "c" in English orthography).

By retaining the *-eme* suffix, *ontolopheme* situates itself within this broader family of terms, signaling that we are addressing a fundamental structural unit – yet with a twist. Unlike graphemes, which are typically examined as abstract markers of phonemes or orthographic positions, ontolophemes emphasize the **conceptual** or **ontic** significance historically tied to each symbol.

A Case for Ontolophemes

1. **Ontos (Being):** In philosophical discourse, *ontos* or *ōn* (ὤν) derives from Ancient Greek ὄντος, "being." It has connotations of existence, essence, and reality (Smith, 2003). By incorporating *ontos* in the term, we evoke the idea that these symbolic units do not merely function as placeholders for linguistic information but embody or *instantiate* aspects of the real world.

2. **Lophos (Crest or Concept):** *Lophos* (λόφος) can mean "crest," "ridge," or, more figuratively, a "summit" of some conceptual domain. In certain extended scholarly uses, *lophos* can denote a conceptual high ground or vantage point, from which the underlying lattice of significance unfolds (Sampson, 1985). Within *ontolopheme*, this element underscores the notion that each letter stands at the "crest" of a conceptual meaning – an apex from which one might glimpse the broader cultural worldview.

3. **-eme (Linguistic Unit):** By retaining the established -*eme* suffix, *ontolopheme* indicates that we are dealing with a **fundamental symbolic unit** within a written system, albeit one layered with extra-linguistic references.

Thus, taken together, *ontolopheme* literally fuses the ideas of **being**, **conceptual crest**, and **fundamental unit**, forming a cohesive term for graphemes that preserve a reference to an object, force, or cosmic principle. Such references often date back to preliterate or early-literate phases when writing systems drew heavily on the environment and spiritual beliefs of their users (Gelb, 1952).

1.2 Core Definition: Graphemes as Fundamental Objects

An **ontolopheme** can be succinctly defined as follows:

An ontolopheme is a grapheme whose shape, name, or cultural usage directly relates to a fundamental concept or "object," reflecting the worldview of the script's originating community.

Crucially, the emphasis here is on the **direct** relationship to an external referent: a tangible or intangible entity that was integral to everyday life or cosmological understanding. For example, a letter that once depicted an **ox** (Aleph/𐤀) or a **fish** (Nun/𐤍), but now appears as an abstract line or curve, might still be considered an ontolopheme insofar as it preserves (however implicitly) that historical connection. The user of modern alphabets (such as English) may no longer perceive the reference to an ox or fish, but textual archaeology and historical linguistics can unveil the archaic link (Cross, 1980).

This definitional framework provides several critical insights:

1. **Historic Genesis**: Ontolophemes often arise in the earliest phases of script development, when writing is more pictorial or logographic. Over time, letters derived from these ontolophemes might become stylized, losing their resemblance to the original object while retaining vestigial references in letter names or symbolic lore (Sass, 1988).

2. **Persistence of Meaning**: Even if contemporary users are unaware of the older signification, the concept remains embedded in the letter's lineage. From the vantage of an esoteric or genealogical perspective, that meaning can be reactivated or studied (Daniels & Bright, 1996).

3. **Cross-Cultural Universality**: The principle of ontolophemes is not exclusive to Semitic alphabets. It applies wherever writing systems have originated in direct references to objects or concepts – be that Egyptian hieroglyphs, Sumerian cuneiform, Chinese

characters, or Mesoamerican scripts (DeFrancis, 1989; Justeson & Stephens, 1994).

With this definition, *ontolopheme* opens a new axis for discussing the function of letters beyond phonetic utility, highlighting their embeddedness in a socio-cultural matrix.

2. Relation to "Logogram," "Pictogram," and "Ideogram"

In traditional linguistics and semiotics, three central terms are often used to describe non-phonetic or partially phonetic signs: **logogram**, **pictogram**, and **ideogram** (Crystal, 2003; DeFrancis, 1989). Each of these labels indicates a different mode of symbolic reference. To situate *ontolopheme* adequately within existing scholarship, we must clarify how it expands upon or intersects with these commonly used classifications.

2.1 Logogram: Word-Level Representation

A **logogram** is a written character that directly represents a single word or morpheme in a given language. Chinese characters, for instance, typically function (at least partly) as logograms, each sign (e.g., 木 for "tree") denoting a discrete lexical item rather than individual phonemes (DeFrancis, 1984). Similarly, Sumerian and Akkadian cuneiform possessed logographic elements where a single sign could mean "king," "god," or "house," among other concepts (Black et al., 2006). From the viewpoint of standard semiotic theory, a logogram is thus **language-specific**: 木 is read as "mù" in Mandarin but might have a different phonetic realization in another Chinese dialect, while the basic conceptual meaning of "tree" remains stable within that language community.

How Ontolophemes Differ:

- **Scope**: An ontolopheme does not necessarily represent a full word; it might correspond to a single letter or phoneme, albeit one that historically derived from a meaningful object. Thus, "A" in English is not a logogram for "ox," but it originated from the shape or reference to an ox (Aleph).

- **Semantic Depth**: Whereas logograms conventionally denote lexical concepts at the word/morpheme level, ontolophemes can originate from an object reference but evolve into purely phonemic usage, preserving the conceptual link genealogically rather than in immediate daily function (Sass, 1988).

In other words, a **logogram** might be read as a *full word* (e.g., "king") in its native script, whereas an ontolopheme can represent a *single phoneme* or letter. Logograms maintain direct semantic content in modern usage, but ontolophemes, especially in alphabets, frequently retain only the *echo* of such content.

2.2 Pictogram: Visual Depiction of an Object

A **pictogram** (or pictograph) is a sign that **visually resembles** the object or concept it represents. Early forms of Egyptian hieroglyphs often verged on pictography, as did the earliest Sumerian cuneiform signs, which might clearly depict a fish, a bird, or a vessel (Gelb, 1952; Manley, 2012). Pictograms thus rely on iconicity: the symbol's shape is intentionally analogous to the referent in the physical or conceptual world.

How Ontolophemes Differ:

- **Iconic vs. Abstract**: An ontolopheme might begin as a pictogram but can become highly abstracted over time. Even if the letter no longer visually resembles the original object, it can still be considered an ontolopheme if historical or etymological evidence links it to that object.

- **Cultural Embedding**: Many pictograms arise in contexts where writing is directly wedded to the environment or a small set of everyday concerns, such as tallying goods or labeling containers (Kramer, 1963). Ontolophemes similarly originate in real-world references but might transform beyond recognizably pictorial forms, retaining the "conceptual crest" within their genealogical name or esoteric usage (Haarmann, 1990).

Thus, while **pictograms** retain an immediate visual similarity to their referent, an **ontolopheme** can lose visual similarity yet persist as a concept-coded symbol. The shape or stylization might evolve drastically, but the conceptual link remains integral to the ontolopheme's historical identity.

2.3 Ideogram: Representation of an Idea or Concept

An **ideogram** designates a graphic symbol that stands for an idea or concept, rather than a specific word or object (Crystal, 2003). For example, a stylized heart shape is widely recognized as symbolizing "love" in Western cultures, even if it bears little resemblance to an anatomical heart. In certain stages of Egyptian writing, some hieroglyphs function purely as ideograms (often called "classifiers" or "determinatives"), clarifying the semantic field of a word without direct phonetic value (Allen, 2014).

How Ontolophemes Differ:

- **Word vs. Concept**: Ideograms typically represent broader ideas or categories (e.g., the notion of "love," "danger," or "male/female") without tying themselves to the morphological specifics of a language. Ontolophemes, however, are intimately connected to a culturally significant object or phenomenon (e.g., an ox, a fish), which might have started as a direct depiction but evolves into a letter that conveys a phoneme in time.

- **Phonetic Shift**: In many esoteric alphabets (e.g., Phoenician, Hebrew, or early Greek), the letter name references an object (Aleph = ox, Beth = house), yet the letter's practical function is to represent a consonant or vowel. That letter is not an ideogram for "ox," but historically emerges from such a reference.

Where **ideograms** might stand for intangible ideas – like "unity," "peace," or "strength" – an ontolopheme is typically anchored in a material or at least concretized referent, one that a community identified as foundational enough to become a building block of their script (Sass, 1988).

2.4 Expanding Standard Linguistic Terminology

In light of these comparisons, the impetus for coining *ontolopheme* becomes clearer: standard categories – logogram, pictogram, ideogram – cannot fully capture the genealogical layering of **letters** that once held direct references to concrete objects or forces but now function purely (or mostly) phonetically. *Ontolopheme* fills this lacuna by emphasizing the **underlying conceptual or cosmological domain** tied to a grapheme's origin, rather than its present use alone (Sampson, 1985).

1. **Temporal Dimension**: Traditional analyses – particularly in synchronic linguistics – often ignore historical layers once a grapheme has become phonetically abstract. *Ontolopheme*, by contrast, legitimizes the significance of genealogical or diachronic ties.

2. **Cultural Embedding**: While logograms, pictograms, and ideograms can sometimes be culturally embedded, the term *ontolopheme* foregrounds cultural anchoring as its defining trait. A letter is recognized as

an ontolopheme if it preserves a memory – through name, shape, or lore – of an object or phenomenon pivotal to its source community (DeFrancis, 1989).

3. **Dynamic Abstraction**: Pictograms or ideograms can remain visually recognizable across centuries (e.g., certain Chinese radicals). However, the alphabetical tradition demonstrates a pattern of **drastic** visual simplification. By referring to letter names (Aleph, Beth, Gimel, Daleth) rather than shapes alone, we see that each letter was once a "semantic capsule" referencing everyday or mythic objects (Sass, 1988).

Hence, in bridging these categories, *ontolopheme* underscores a synergy: it acknowledges how a single sign can begin as a pictogram, evolve away from iconic depiction, and function as a phoneme marker – yet still harbor conceptual significance due to its intangible link to an older worldview.

2.5 Illustrative Example: Aleph as an Ontolopheme

To illustrate how an ontolopheme might diverge from logograms, pictograms, or ideograms, consider **Aleph (𐤀)** in the Phoenician script, the direct ancestor of Greek **Alpha** (A) and Latin **A**. Historically, Aleph is believed to derive from a stylized representation of an ox head, connecting to pastoral economies that prized livestock (Cross, 1980). As a letter, Aleph quickly morphed into a sign representing the glottal stop or an initial vowel in Semitic languages. Its shape no longer clearly resembled an ox's head, and it functioned within the script as a consonant or place-holder for a vowel – **not** as a discrete word meaning "ox."

- **Not a Logogram**: Aleph is not read as "ox" in the same sense that a Chinese logogram might be read as "牛" (niú) meaning "cow" or "ox." Instead, Aleph simply represents a phoneme.

- **Not a Pure Pictogram**: Over time, the shape lost its pictorial dimension; in the Roman letter "A," the stylized version is more triangular, typically with a crossbar. Only through historical-linguistic analysis can we confirm its origin as an ox's head.

- **Not an Ideogram**: Aleph does not stand for the idea of "ox-ness" or "animal strength" in a general sense. Rather, it references an ox specifically as an anchor for a phoneme symbol, rooted in a farming society's environment.

Yet, by the logic of ontolophemes, Aleph retains a genealogical tie to the concept of an ox. Its letter name and earliest inscriptions confirm this link, even though the modern user no longer harnesses it for that meaning (Daniels & Bright, 1996). This exemplifies the *ontolopheme* dynamic: the letter derived from an "ontic seed" but transformed into an abstract sign, bridging pragmatic phonetics and archaic significance.

2.6 Cosmic or Cosmological Domains

Another distinction that *ontolopheme* brings into relief is the capacity for certain letters to encode **cosmological** or **mythic** domains, not solely tangible objects. While many early letters were grounded in the material realities of pastoral life, some writing systems also included signs referencing intangible forces or deities. For instance, in Egyptian hieroglyphs, signs referencing cosmic entities like the sun disk (Ra) or "sky" (represented often by the sky-goddess Nut) were sometimes integrated into texts (Manley, 2012). If an alphabetic letter subsequently emerged from such a glyph – though no direct, widely recognized example may exist – it would stand as an ontolopheme of a different sort: bridging intangible cosmic concepts rather than physical objects.

Historically, Semitic alphabets are typically said to revolve around **everyday references**: "house," "hand," "fish," "tooth," etc. (Sass, 1988). Still, there may be overshadowed or lesser-documented examples of letters referencing more abstract or mythic matters (Haarmann, 1990). In that scenario, an ontolopheme might correspond to an ancient religious symbol or supernatural entity, carrying forward a vestigial cosmic association. Although verifying such claims often proves challenging due to limited epigraphic data, the theoretical framework of ontolophemes permits such interpretations, so long as historical evidence connects a given grapheme to an intangible concept within the script's originating culture.

2.7 Practical Implications for Research and Education

By offering a vantage that transcends standard semiotic categories, *ontolopheme* provides a robust tool for both **research** and **pedagogy**.

Research:

- **Archaeological Epigraphy**: Scholars analyzing early inscriptions can apply the lens of ontolophemes to identify which letters carry references to material or cosmic domains. This helps differentiate purely adapted phonetic symbols from those that functioned as culturally significant anchors (Cross, 1980).

- **Comparative Mythology**: Linguists and mythographers might collaborate to see how certain objects – like oxen, fish, or houses – emerge as recurring ontic seeds across multiple script traditions (Daniels & Bright, 1996). The concept of ontolophemes streamlines that discourse by highlighting genealogical continuity.

Education:

- **Literacy and Historical Awareness**: Presenting alphabets as a historically layered phenomenon fosters a more engaging learning experience for students. Instead of rote memorization of letters, learners discover that "A" once represented an ox, "B" a house, and so forth (Crystal, 2003). This approach can kindle curiosity about cultural evolution and deepen respect for the interplay between speech, writing, and environment.

- **Conlang Development**: Constructed language (conlang) creators often invest their scripts with deliberate symbolic references (Peterson, 2015). The notion of ontolophemes provides a theoretical scaffolding for them to craft letters that double as reflections of a fictional culture's daily realities or spiritual beliefs.

2.8 Relevance in a Modern Context

Even if the majority of contemporary literacy practices treat letters as inert shapes correlating to phonemes, acknowledging the ontolopheme dimension can **re-enchant** our relationship with writing (Haarmann, 1990). Instead of perceiving "B" or "C" as purely arbitrary lines, we might sense the latent echoes of an older worldview. This resonates with broader movements in cultural studies and heritage preservation, where the emphasis is on unearthing intangible histories lodged in artifacts and textual remains (Smith, 2003).

Digital mediums – where letters are typed and transmitted at lightning speed – may seem to accelerate the decontextualization of graphemes. However, new technologies also enable unprecedented cross-referencing of script histories, genealogies, and morphological transformations (Crystal, 2003). Automated systems can link a letter in a text to a reference page explaining its archaic meaning. In such an environment, *ontolopheme* stands as a clarifying concept, encouraging scholars and developers alike to integrate historical references into digital writing platforms, bridging the ephemeral nature of modern communication with the profound lineage of each letter.

2.9 Summary: A Fresh Paradigm for Letter Study

In sum, *ontolopheme* expands upon logogram, pictogram, and ideogram by foregrounding the **historical and conceptual** significance of a grapheme, even when it no longer visually depicts or semantically denotes the object from which it arose. Unlike a logogram, an ontolopheme need not represent a complete word. Unlike a pictogram, it can diverge drastically from its original image. And unlike an ideogram, it might not denote an abstract idea but a very specific object or cosmic principle. Its essence is genealogical: a living or vestigial link to the cultural "seed" that birthed it.

This framework resonates with the earlier exploration of alphabets as ontologies (Section II.A). Seeing letters through the lens of ontolophemes allows us to integrate **esoteric** notions, historical–linguistic evidence, and structural theories of writing systems (Sampson, 1985). Just as each letter in a Phoenician-based script once corresponded to an object (Aleph = ox, Beth = house, Gimel = camel, Daleth = door), so too might those associations remain latent even after centuries of abstraction (Daniels & Bright, 1996). The coinage of *ontolopheme* thus offers a precise term for the phenomenon whereby each grapheme stands at the crest (*lophos*) of being (*ontos*), bridging the realm of practical phonetic function and ancestral conceptual depth.

The ramifications for modern scholarship are considerable. Rather than confining letters to a purely phonetic role, future studies may incorporate their genealogical histories and symbolic associations. Such an approach fosters interdisciplinary dialogue among **linguists, epigraphers, anthropologists**, and **mythologists** – all of whom have a stake in understanding the multi-layered significance of textual symbols. Furthermore, educators and conlang enthusiasts gain a conceptual tool to reanimate the learning or creation of scripts, thereby reintegrating writing systems with the living or mythic worlds they once served to index.

C. Sacred Geometry and the Alphabet

The English alphabet, on first inspection, appears simply as a repertoire of twenty-six letters – functional symbols used to record speech. Yet, upon deeper investigation, these graphemes reveal hidden genealogical layers connected to ancient pictographic or conceptual roots (Sampson, 1985). The **sacred geometry** approach interprets alphabets through a **polygonal metaphor**, symbolizing how writing systems can be envisioned as bounded shapes, each "side" representing a discrete letter or conceptual lineage. Two polygons, in particular, serve as focal points for understanding the modern English script's evolution and hidden ontology: the **icosikaihexagon (26 sides)**, which parallels the exoteric usage of our current alphabet, and the **icosihenagon (21 sides)**, evoking the genealogical or esoteric substrate from which many of these letters derive (Cross, 1980; Daniels & Bright, 1996).

1. Icosikaihexagon (26 Sides)

1.1 The English Alphabet as an Exoteric Form

In contemporary English orthography, the letters **A** through **Z** stand in neat rows on children's classroom walls, grace the pages of spelling books, and shape our daily digital communications (Crystal, 2003). We rarely pause to consider that this 26-letter sequence is a historical product of centuries of adaptation, standardization, and borrowing – from Greek to Etruscan to Latin, and eventually to medieval and modern English usage (Sampson, 1985). Nevertheless, for the average speaker, these letters form a stable, taken-for-granted system.

The **icosikaihexagon** is a metaphor that captures this stable arrangement: a polygon with **26 sides**, each side representing one letter in our exoteric alphabet. Within the metaphorical plane, each side is distinct and equally visible, symbolizing how the English alphabet is taught as a uniform set of discrete graphemes. At face value, such a polygon neatly corresponds to the **exoteric** dimension of English letters – where each grapheme is typically understood as a vehicle for one or more phonemes. This vantage is heavily influenced by modern linguistics, which focuses on the phonetic or morphological roles of letters (Crystal, 2003).

1.1.1 Historical Expansion into 26 Letters

Historically, the Roman alphabet inherited by Old English contained fewer letters. Latin's reliance on **U, V, and sometimes W** (initially all represented by V) eventually expanded into distinct graphemes in English, due in part to the need to represent the **/u/, /v/,** and **/w/** phonemes (Daniels & Bright, 1996). Similarly, the letter **J** diverged from **I** to capture the /dʒ/ or /j/ sound, and even **Y** traces its lineage back to Greek **Upsilon** but took on new roles in English, sometimes representing /j/ or /ɪ/ (Sampson, 1985). The net result: a final set of 26 letters that can be enumerated, displayed, and memorized with relative simplicity. Each letter, in the classroom sense, is a distinct "edge" or "angle" of the exoteric polygon – recognized in its own right without immediate reference to hidden genealogies.

1.1.2 Function vs. Form

Conceived as an **icosikaihexagon**, the English alphabet's **function** is primarily to transcribe spoken English. Modern orthography, though riddled with historical inconsistencies, remains serviceable enough to capture the broad inventory of English phonemes. Each letter's **form** is standardized to a recognizable shape across printing conventions (e.g., "A" as an uppercase triangle with a crossbar, "B" as vertical strokes connected by two loops), or a variant in cursive or typed fonts. The exoteric dimension thus emphasizes mechanical clarity:

A Case for Ontolophemes

- **A** spells /æ/ or /eɪ/, among other realizations depending on context.

- **B** spells /b/.

- **C** can represent /k/ or /s/ depending on subsequent letters (e.g., "cake" vs. "cite").

These details, from a purely functional standpoint, obscure the deeper story behind how "A" might once have depicted an **ox** or how "C" can be traced back to **Gamma**, referencing a "camel" in Phoenician (Cross, 1980). Within the icosikaihexagon perspective, such genealogical nuance is rarely foregrounded. Instead, the letter's present usage is the main focus.

1.1.3 Advantages of the Polygon Metaphor

Envisioning the English alphabet as a **26-sided polygon** underscores the idea of **bounded completeness** – the impression that all necessary signs for English appear in a closed set. Much as a geometric figure encloses space with a finite number of edges, so too does the alphabet supply a comprehensive set of graphemes for encoding most words in the language (Crystal, 2003). The polygonal shape also implies an **equal weighting** to each letter, an exoteric stance wherein "A" and "Z" stand as symmetrical extremes, everything in between forming a continuum. In practical usage, we do not typically ascribe deeper meaning to the shapes or historical connotations behind these letters – only to their function. Teachers recite the alphabet song from "A, B, C" to "X, Y, Z," each letter given a uniform highlight.

Therefore, the notion of an **icosikaihexagon** addresses how **English is taught, learned, and conceptually grasped** at a surface level. Each grapheme is seen as an **independent side**, a distinct tool in the orthographic kit, with minimal reflection on ancestral significance or conceptual roots. Such an outlook, while incomplete from a historical or esoteric vantage, is highly practical for everyday literacy.

2. Icosihenagon (21 Sides)

In contrast to the exoteric perspective of 26 discrete letters, the **esoteric** or genealogical perspective unveils a more compact and conceptually unified *inner geometry*. Various lines of philological and epigraphic evidence suggest that the letters in the English alphabet do not all trace back to 26 unique ancient roots. Rather, by tracking the lineages of letters – especially in the Phoenician or early Semitic scripts that shaped Greek and Latin – one finds **overlapping** or **duplicated** genealogies (Sass, 1988). When these duplications are discounted, a consistent figure of around **21 core objects** or conceptual references emerges, forming what we might call the **icosihenagon** – a 21-sided polygon representing the fundamental ontic seeds behind our modern graphemes (Daniels & Bright, 1996).

2.1 Hidden Genealogical Blueprint

The key to uncovering this **hidden blueprint** lies in recognizing that many Roman letters share a common ancestral Phoenician glyph. For instance, from the Phoenician letter **Waw** (𐤅, "hook/peg"), we ultimately derive **U, V, W**, and even **Y** in certain lineages (Cross, 1980). Similarly, from Phoenician **Yod** (𐤉, "hand" or "arm"), both **I** and **J** emerged, while the letter **G** was created as a modified form of **C** in Latin to differentiate /g/ from /k/ (Sampson, 1985). These expansions and branchings, though they yield distinct letters in modern usage, do not necessarily reflect distinct original concepts. They represent a single ancestral root diversified through orthographic and phonological pressures over time (Sass, 1988).

In other words, while the icosikaihexagon is the outward shape we see in English, the icosihenagon captures the deeper reality: multiple modern letters can converge on the **same** archaic "ontolopheme." The letter name and shape that once signified a "hook," "arm," or "camel" might now pro-

A Case for Ontolophemes

duce two, three, or even four distinct graphemes. Stripping away these branched duplications returns us to a more integral set of about 21 items – coinciding with the original repertoire that Phoenician scripts carried forward from proto-Canaanite traditions (Cross, 1980).

2.1.1 Examples of Duplications

1. U, V, W, Y:
   - All trace to Phoenician **Waw** (𐤅), typically glossed as "hook" or "peg," possibly referencing a peg used in tents or building.
   - Latin did not differentiate between vowel /u/ and consonantal /v/ initially, so the same letter "V" served both roles. Later, "U" emerged for the vowel, "V" for the consonant, "W" for a double-u or /w/ sound, and "Y" sometimes integrated from Greek *Upsilon*.
   - Thus, four English letters revolve around a single ontic concept: a "peg," an ordinary object in desert or pastoral societies that built portable structures (Sass, 1988).

2. I, J:
   - Both historically trace back to **Yod** (𐤉), meaning "hand/arm." Although they now represent separate sounds in English, their genealogical link underscores that only one original "hand" glyph existed in Phoenician scripts (Sampson, 1985).

3. C, G:
   - In early Latin, "C" could represent both /k/ and /g/. A diacritic or additional stroke eventually led to the letter "G," splitting the phonemic distinction into two letters. Yet, from a

genealogical stance, both letters hail from a single Phoenician glyph: **Gimel** (𐤂), referencing a "camel" (Cross, 1980).

These examples illuminate how the **26** exoteric letters can be whittled down once we acknowledge their shared origins. From a genealogical standpoint, these duplications do not alter the fact that each letter might have a unique function in modern English; they simply highlight that the actual number of *proto-concepts* behind the letters is smaller – **21** rather than 26.

2.2 Core Concepts in the "Inner Geometry"

If one systematically removes duplications and merges lineages, around **21 fundamental referents** typically remain – often paralleling the original 22-letter Phoenician script minus certain local variations (Daniels & Bright, 1996). While scholars might disagree on the precise tally due to ambiguities in letter histories (e.g., debate over the exact meaning of Qoph or Samekh), a consistent list emerges that references items critical to ancient agrarian or pastoral life (Cross, 1980). These items often include:

1. **Aleph (𐤀):** "Ox," symbolizing strength and sustenance.

2. **Beth (𐤁):** "House," signifying shelter or domesticity.

3. **Gimel (𐤂):** "Camel," a crucial beast of burden in Semitic societies.

4. **Daleth (𐤃):** "Door," a boundary or threshold.

5. **He (𐤄):** Sometimes "window" or "breath," connoting openness.

A Case for Ontolophemes

6. **Waw (𐤅):** "Hook" or "peg," referencing tent structures.

7. **Zayin (𐤆):** "Weapon" or "sword," capturing martial or protective power.

8. **Heth (𐤇):** "Fence," marking an enclosure.

9. **Teth (𐤈):** Possibly "wheel" or a shape referencing a "basket," though debated.

10. **Yod (𐤉):** "Hand" or "arm," signifying action and craftsmanship.

11. **Kaph (𐤊):** "Palm (of the hand)," extension of manual function.

12. **Lamedh (𐤋):** "Goad/cattle prod," connoting control or direction.

13. **Mem (𐤌):** "Water," essential for survival and symbolic of chaos or life.

14. **Nun (𐤍):** "Fish," another staple or symbol of fertility.

15. **Samekh (𐤎):** Possibly "spine" or "support," though interpretations vary.

16. **Ayin (𐤏):** "Eye," referencing vision or awareness.

17. **Pe (𐤐):** "Mouth," alluding to speech or consumption.

18. **Sadhe (𐤑):** "Plant or papyrus," or an angled shape denoting a snare, also debated.

19. **Qoph (𐤒):** Possibly "monkey," "back of the head," or "needle's eye."

20. **Resh (𐤓):** "Head," embodying leadership or the top of the body.

Icosikaihexagon and Icosihenagon

21. **Shin (W):** "Tooth," referencing biting or devouring power.

22. **Taw (+):** "Mark" or "cross," a sign of boundary or identity.

Not all of these correspond perfectly to the modern English 26 letters, and certain letters in the Latin script have no direct Phoenician counterpart (e.g., English's "J," "U," "W," are expansions). By removing overlaps and focusing on the conceptual "progenitors," we see how the script can be reduced from an exoteric 26 to an esoteric 21 or 22. The **icosihenagon** thus signifies that the script, at its genealogical core, is more unified and conceptually condensed than the surface 26 might suggest (Sass, 1988).

2.2.1 Archetypal Objects and Concepts

The listed referents – ox, house, fish, water, eye, mouth, etc. – often reflect staples of everyday existence in Bronze Age Levantine societies (Cross, 1980). Domestic animals, essential architecture, resources for nourishment, and bodily organs appear repeatedly. These items collectively **form the "ontological cosmos"** of that environment: where an ox is critical for plowing, a house for shelter, water for irrigation, and fish a dietary staple. Such references are not arbitrary but indicative of what was central to survival and identity (Gelb, 1952). Over time, as scripts moved into Greek and Latin contexts, the pragmatic memory of these references receded, replaced by emphasis on phonetic usage. However, the letter names or morphological vestiges serve as historical fingerprints, confirming the deeper genealogical substrate.

2.2.2 Morphological Distortions Over Time

In the journey from proto-Canaanite to Phoenician, to Greek, to Etruscan, and finally to Latin, the shapes of the letters underwent **progressive stylization**. The "ox head" or "house plan" might become geometric lines, losing direct pictorial resonance (Sampson, 1985). But the letter names and evidence from epigraphy affirm that these shapes once functioned as pictographs or semantically meaningful glyphs (DeFrancis, 1989). By the time of English usage, letters like "A" or "M" appear purely abstract. Only through genealogical study do we rediscover that "A" might link back to an ox's head (Aleph) and "M" to water (Mem). This morphological distortion underlies the reason why modern observers rarely see a "house" in "B" or a "door" in "D," though historical linguistics places those associations at the script's root (Cross, 1980).

Thus, the **icosihenagon** stands as a conceptual tool for capturing these original references, ensuring we do not conflate expansions or purely phonetic duplications with wholly separate genealogical items. It serves as an "inner geometry" that reveals the script's underlying order – 21 or so prime concepts – beneath the exoteric 26 letters of modern English usage.

2.3 The Sacred Dimension of Inner Geometry

Why characterize this genealogical blueprint as "sacred geometry"? The term "sacred geometry" classically refers to **geometric patterns** (e.g., circles, triangles, spirals) that embody cosmic or divine principles in the worldview of various spiritual traditions (Lawlor, 1982). Applying such language to the alphabet conveys that these letters, at their origin, were not purely functional placeholders for phonemes, but **ontolophemes** – units imbued with conceptual or mythic weight (Haarmann, 1990). The "sacred" element, in this sense, arises from:

1. **Ancestral Priority**: The fundamental objects – oxen, water, houses, fish – were cornerstones of life, survival, and possibly religious symbolism (Sass, 1988).

2. **Cosmic Integration**: Letters like "eye" (Ayin) or "head" (Resh) reflect not just physical objects but philosophical or spiritual vantage points (vision, cognition).

3. **Integration in Ritual**: In some ancient contexts, scribes and priests used letters in amulets, incantations, or sacred inscriptions. Each letter may have served as an invocation of the object or force it represented (Manley, 2012).

From this standpoint, the **icosihenagon** is akin to an **inner mandala** or blueprint, uniting daily realities (agriculture, herding, building) with intangible spiritual or cosmic forces. While modern orthography typically severs these associations, their historical resonance persists, and the geometric metaphor helps illustrate how these 21 "sides" fit together into a coherent conceptual mosaic.

2.4 Contrasting the Two Polygons: Exoteric vs. Esoteric

To summarize:

1. Exoteric Icosikaihexagon (26 Sides):
    - Reflects the present, widely recognized set of English letters.
    - Each letter is treated as an independent entity, assigned to transcribe certain sounds.
    - Stems from centuries of expansions, splits (e.g., U/V/W/Y), and morphological changes.
    - Aligns with standard teaching methods that introduce children to "A, B, C ... X, Y, Z" as a finite list of graphemes.

2. Esoteric Icosihenagon (21 Sides):

A Case for Ontolophemes

- Reflects the deeper genealogical and symbolic substrate behind those letters.
- Emphasizes that multiple letters share single ancestral ontic units (e.g., Yod → I/J, Waw → U/V/W/Y).
- Centers on about 21 fundamental objects or references – an "inner geometry" that organizes the script's original conceptual domain.
- Evokes a sense of "sacred geometry," as each letter once intersected with vital aspects of ancient life, bridging everyday experience and cosmic perception.

The interplay between these two perspectives underscores a **dual nature** of the English alphabet: it is simultaneously a pragmatic code for modern communication and a repository of archaic conceptual linkages. Recognizing the icosihenagon – an ontological blueprint – reminds us that alphabets, though they may appear superficial or purely phonetic in our daily usage, can also function as living legacies of older civilizations (Cross, 1980).

2.5 Significance for Linguistic and Cultural Studies

Elucidating the icosihenagon phenomenon enriches **linguistic and cultural studies** by demonstrating that orthographic expansions do not necessarily equate to expansions of conceptual content. Indeed, the English alphabet is "bigger" than its Phoenician ancestor, but genealogically it does not encode more fundamental objects – simply more specialized letters derived from shared roots (Sass, 1988). This has implications for:

1. **Language Teaching**: Educators might incorporate genealogical tidbits when introducing letters, thereby expanding students' awareness beyond the typical

functional approach. Knowing that "B" derives from "house" (Beth) and "D" from "door" (Daleth) could foster curiosity about historical transitions and comparative alphabets (Crystal, 2003).

2. **Comparative Script Research**: Scholars analyzing the expansions of the Roman alphabet could benefit from the icosihenagon lens, differentiating truly distinct genealogical lines from phonetic splits. This fosters clarity in discussing which letters represent new conceptual additions and which represent diversification of older ones (Daniels & Bright, 1996).

3. **Cultural Symbolism**: The "inner geometry" illuminates how, in a time when writing was intimately connected to daily survival and spiritual beliefs, each letter might have functioned as an invocation of farmland, livestock, home, or cosmic principle. Modern usage often bypasses that dimension, but genealogical research can help recover it for cultural or even liturgical renewal (Haarmann, 1990).

2.6 Relevance to the Ontolopheme Concept

The metaphors of the **icosikaihexagon** and **icosihenagon** dovetail seamlessly with the idea of **ontolophemes** (Section II.B). Each side of the esoteric icosihenagon corresponds to a unique ontolopheme in the sense that it references a distinct concept (e.g., "ox," "house," "camel," "fish"). By contrast, the exoteric icosikaihexagon lumps multiple derived letters under separate headings – like U, V, W, Y for a single root glyph. This mismatch reveals how the same ontolopheme can spawn several graphemes in modern alphabets, reinforcing the distinction between an alphabet's **functional** expansions and its **ontological** or genealogical essence (DeFrancis, 1989).

A Case for Ontolophemes

When analyzing "A, B, C, D, ..." as purely 26 letters, we risk overlooking that "A" (Aleph) and "G" (once part of "C") are genealogically distinct, while "V" and "U" share the same origin (Waw). The ontolopheme framework prompts scholars to discern **which** letters have genuine distinct ancestry and which are offshoots of the same conceptual seed (Sass, 1988). This fosters a more nuanced reading of the English script, bridging the practicality of daily spelling with a recognition of deeper historical multiplicities.

2.7 Future Directions

The interplay of geometry and genealogy in analyzing alphabets can have several ramifications for future research:

- **Digital Visualization**: Modern technologies could map each letter to its ancestor in a graphical interface, illustrating the branching expansions that lead from a single Phoenician glyph (e.g., Waw) to multiple English letters (U, V, W, Y). A "dynamic polygon" might show edges splitting or merging over time, echoing how the script's expansions relate to morphological innovations.

- **Cross-Linguistic Comparisons**: The approach that identifies an inner geometry of 21 or 22 concepts could be compared with other alphabets or abjads (e.g., Aramaic, Hebrew, Arabic) to see whether a similar tension exists between exoteric letter sets and esoteric genealogies (Sampson, 1985).

- **Interdisciplinary Studies**: Anthropologists or mythographers might track how these fundamental referents – ox, house, fish, water – persist not just in script but in cultural rituals, folktales, or religious rites, revealing the synergy between textual representation and living tradition (Cross, 1980).

Icosikaihexagon and Icosihenagon

Ultimately, the **sacred geometry** lens underscores that alphabets are rarely random collections of symbols: they often reflect deeper, integrative patterns shaped by environmental needs, spiritual frameworks, and historical expansions (Gelb, 1952). The icosikaihexagon and icosihenagon metaphors highlight how a modern script might look "complete" at 26 letters while actually resting on a narrower conceptual foundation of around 21 prime ontolophemes.

Concluding Reflections

Viewed through **sacred geometry**, the English alphabet stands as a **dual structure**: an **exoteric** icosikaihexagon of 26 distinct letters and an **esoteric** icosihenagon linking back to 21 ancestral referents. This duality epitomizes how writing systems evolve – expanding and branching to accommodate new phonemic distinctions or orthographic conventions – yet remain moored to older symbolic frameworks. Though modern learners seldom realize that "V" and "U" both stem from a single hook/peg concept, or that "I" and "J" share the same "hand" lineage, philological evidence reveals a genealogical compression at writing's roots (Daniels & Bright, 1996; Sass, 1988).

Understanding the icosihenagon, or the "inner geometry," fosters a **re-enchantment** of the alphabet: a recognition that letters are not mere inert tools but living memorials of how ancient societies conceptualized their world – complete with domestic animals, housing structures, water sources, and intangible forces like crossing marks or eyes. The notion of *ontolophemes* deepens this perspective, showing that each letter in an older script could be an ontic unit bridging speech, livelihood, and spiritual significance (Haarmann, 1990).

Hence, the interplay between **26** and **21** is not trivial: it highlights the difference between surface-level function

A Case for Ontolophemes

and deeper genealogical meaning. The exoteric polygon sits on every school desk and is recited in every alphabet song, while the esoteric one lies hidden behind centuries of adaptation, waiting for textual archaeology and symbolic interpretation to bring it back into focus. Far from a mere academic curiosity, this approach to **sacred geometry** in script invites us to rediscover the storied heritage in each letter we write or read, bridging the daily act of spelling with an ancient lattice of objects, livelihoods, and cosmic resonances.

Icosikaihexagon and Icosihenagon

III. GENEALOGY OF THE ENGLISH ALPHABET

A. From Proto-Sinaitic to Phoenician

The modern English alphabet – an unassuming row of 26 letters on classroom walls and in countless books – traces back to multiple historical scripts. Among these ancestral roots, none are more pivotal than the early Semitic writing systems typically referred to as **Proto-Sinaitic** and their subsequent adaptation into **Phoenician**. Together, they provided the template for alphabets across the Mediterranean, ultimately influencing Greek, Latin, and the scripts that followed (Daniels & Bright, 1996). This section delves into how a once-limited set of pictographic signs in the Sinai region transformed into a streamlined, 22-letter system that encoded the core objects and realities of ancient Levantine society.

1. Proto-Sinaitic Origins

1.1 Early Pictographs: Local Objects and Daily Life

The term **Proto-Sinaitic** refers to a group of inscriptions discovered mainly in the **Sinai Peninsula**, particularly around sites such as **Serabit el-Khadim**, where turquoise mines and related Egyptian outposts were active during the **Middle Kingdom** and **Second Intermediate Period** (ca. 1900–1500 BCE). Scholars first recognized these inscriptions in the early 20th century, noting that some of the signs seemed loosely derived from **Egyptian hieroglyphs** yet functioned differently (Sass, 1988; DeFrancis, 1989). Unlike the elaborate Egyptian system – which employed hundreds of glyphs in both logographic and phonetic roles – Proto-Sinaitic inscriptions hinted at a more compressed repertoire of pictographs, each standing for a **consonantal** sound in a proto-Semitic language (Cross, 1980).

Icosikaihexagon and Icosihenagon

1.1.1 Archaeological Context

Archaeologists generally concur that Semitic-speaking laborers, possibly employed by or interacting with Egyptian overseers, adapted certain Egyptian signs to represent Semitic consonants. These workers likely had reasons to create a simplified script, whether for **inventory recording**, **personal inscriptions**, or **religious dedications** at local shrines (Manley, 2012). The environment of Serabit el-Khadim – where turquoise mining led to an intersection of Egyptian administration and local labor forces – offered fertile ground for linguistic cross-pollination. Egyptian hieroglyphs were visible on temple reliefs and stelae, while the Semites presumably needed a more accessible means to jot down names or short statements in their own tongue (Sass, 1988).

Amid these cultural exchanges, certain Egyptian glyphs – like a **head, a snake, a doorway** – were **repurposed** or **reinterpreted** to capture the initial consonant of their Semitic names. This appropriation laid the groundwork for an **acrophonic principle**: the sign for "house" (in the Semitic language) might have been used to denote the consonant /b/, derived from the first sound of the Semitic word for "house" (e.g., bayt). Such an approach drastically simplified the writing system, reducing it to a small set of symbols – potentially between 20 and 30 – adequate for capturing the consonantal skeleton of the Semitic speech stream (Sampson, 1985).

1.1.2 Pictographic Roots and Local References

While firm readings of Proto-Sinaitic inscriptions remain challenging due to their brevity and limited archaeological attestation, paleographic analysis reveals that many signs were originally **pictographic** – that is, they had shapes resembling everyday objects or environment-specific items (Sass, 1988). These pictographs included (but were not limited to):

A Case for Ontolophemes

- **Ox head or bull's head**: A sign that would eventually evolve into Phoenician Aleph (𐤀).

- **House or rectangular plan**: Possibly a sign leading to Beth (𐤁).

- A form of throwing stick or curved line: Possibly Gimel (𐤂).

- **A doorway**: Anticipating Daleth (𐤃).

These depictions reflect **local objects and daily life** among Semitic groups in the Sinai. Herding animals, rudimentary dwellings, and implements for hunting or mining formed the backdrop of everyday survival. The scribes who adapted these glyphs were thus selecting symbols with direct relevance to their environment – oxen for plowing or nourishment, houses for familial identity, tools for labor (Cross, 1980). In so doing, they turned the script into a compressed **ontology** of crucial resources and concepts, even if the system was still in embryonic form.

It is significant to note that **Egyptian hieroglyphs** themselves also originated in pictographic representations. Yet, while the Egyptian script grew into a complex synergy of logograms, phonograms, and determinatives, Proto-Sinaitic branched off toward a more **phonemic** or consonantal path. This divergence underscores the innovative step of **reducing** the script to a minimal set of **consonant signs**, making it more portable and easier to learn for speakers of Semitic languages (DeFrancis, 1989). The impetus for this reduction – some argue – was a desire for straightforward record-keeping among individuals less trained in the advanced scribal traditions of Egypt, or perhaps simply a matter of practicality amid frontier conditions in the Sinai mines (Haarmann, 1990).

1.2 Emergence of a Simplified Sign System for Consonants

1.2.1 Acrophonic Principle and Consonantal Representation

The **acrophonic principle** is central to Proto-Sinaitic's significance: each pictograph stood for the **initial consonant** of its Semitic name (Cross, 1980). If the pictograph was recognized as a "fish" (likely the Semitic word "nun"), it was used to represent /n/. If it depicted a "water" symbol (perhaps "mem" in Semitic), it symbolized /m/. This method contrasts with Egyptian writing, which might use a fish glyph as either a logogram for "fish" or as a phonogram for certain syllables, but not consistently as a single consonant (Sass, 1988).

Moreover, Proto-Sinaitic signs were used predominantly for **consonants**, likely because Semitic languages place significant morphological weight on consonantal roots, with vowels serving more flexible grammatical or syntactic roles (DeFrancis, 1989). By capturing consonants alone, the script could form the backbone of words and rely on reader familiarity to infer the missing vowel patterns – an approach eventually codified in the **abjad** systems of Phoenician, Aramaic, and Hebrew.

1.2.2 Limited Corpus and Scholarly Debates

Despite Proto-Sinaitic's recognized status as a crucial transitional script, the **corpus** of inscriptions is small and often cryptic, leading to ongoing debates over specific sign identifications, phonetic values, and translations (Sass, 1988). Scholars like Cross (1980) and DeFrancis (1989) highlight that while the broad outlines of acrophony are widely accepted, disagreements linger about particular glyphs. For instance, does a certain sign truly represent "door," or might it reflect another local object? Are certain inscriptions from

A Case for Ontolophemes

Serabit el-Khadim purely decorative or might they carry short dedicatory phrases to a local deity?

Nevertheless, a near consensus persists on the general trajectory: a set of pictorial symbols referencing local objects and daily life coalesced into a **simplified sign system** focusing on consonants, bridging Egyptian influence and Semitic usage. This system would eventually, through further shaping and standardization, evolve into the **Proto-Canaanite** script and ultimately the **Phoenician** alphabet. Within this lineage, Proto-Sinaitic stands as the earliest known attempt to unify pictorial signs into a manageable, phonemically oriented script (Haarmann, 1990).

2. Phoenician as the Major Turning Point

While Proto-Sinaitic laid the groundwork, the **Phoenician** script represents a monumental **turning point** in the history of alphabetic writing (Daniels & Bright, 1996). Often hailed as the first extensively attested alphabet (as opposed to a syllabary or complex logographic system), Phoenician effectively crystallized the approach glimpsed in Proto-Sinaitic. It refined and standardized a repertoire of **22 consonant signs**, each bearing a name that pointed to a tangible object or concept integral to Levantine life (Sass, 1988). The Phoenician script would soon diffuse around the Mediterranean world via trade networks, profoundly impacting the development of Greek, Latin, and in due course, the alphabets of modern Europe.

2.1 The 22-Letter Script Named After Real-World Items

2.1.1 Structured Abjad with Consistent Consonant Values

Building on the acrophonic principle, **Phoenician** formalized a set of 22 letters – Aleph (✦), Beth (ϑ), Gimel (ᒣ), Daleth (ᐊ), He (ᔕ), Waw (ᔨ), Zayin (ᒐ), Heth (ᗗ), Teth (⊕), Yod (ᔓ), Kaph (ᐅ), Lamedh (ᒪ), Mem (ᕐ), Nun (ᕐ),

Samekh (𐤎), Ayin (𐤏), Pe (𐤐), Sadhe (𐤑), Qoph (𐤒), Resh (𐤓), Shin (𐤔), and Taw (𐤕). Each letter's **name** was that of an **object**, typically referencing daily or cosmic realities:

- **Aleph** (𐤀) meant "ox," underscoring the region's agrarian or pastoral economy (Cross, 1980).

- **Beth** (𐤁) signified "house," pointing to the structure fundamental to domestic life.

- **Gimel** (𐤂) was a "camel," an indispensable beast of burden in desert trade routes.

- **Daleth** (𐤃) connoted a "door," an immediate part of any physical dwelling.

Such naming offered more than a mnemonic device: it *enshrined* each letter's connection to a tangible or even sacral concept, forging a direct link between script and environment. The 22 consonants, collectively, enabled robust representation of the basic phonemic structure of the Canaanite dialects (Sass, 1988).

2.1.2 Expansion of the Levantine "Vocabulary"

By listing each letter as a **real-world item**, the Phoenician script effectively compiled a **miniature vocabulary** representing everyday, pragmatic, and sometimes spiritual phenomena. The resulting synergy meant that each letter was not merely a phonetic token but also a conceptual token. When scribes used Daleth for the /d/ sound, they were implicitly acknowledging the letter's reference to "door," a boundary that shaped daily life in walled cities or simple dwellings of the Levant (Daniels & Bright, 1996). In essence, the Phoenician alphabet formed an **ontology** of the region: oxen, houses, camels, fish, water, the mouth, the eye, and more. Each grapheme was an **ontolopheme** – a letter intimately linked to a conceptual domain vital to that civilization (Cross, 1980).

A Case for Ontolophemes

This anchoring in **local reality** highlights the synergy between language and environment. The territory of the Levant encompassed farmland suitable for livestock, proximity to the Mediterranean for trade, and a climate where shelters, wells, and city gates were central to daily survival. The **Phoenicians** themselves – renowned sailors and traders – were accustomed to forging connections across coastal cities (Tyre, Sidon, Byblos) and beyond. Thus, their script mirrored the region's commercial, domestic, and agrarian bedrock while facilitating record-keeping, maritime trade, and correspondence (Sass, 1988).

2.2 How These Names Enshrined a Cosmic or Territorial "Vocabulary"

2.2.1 Enrichment Beyond Simple Phonetics

Many treat the Phoenician letters purely as **phonetic** building blocks – an abjad for writing Canaanite languages. However, the significance of naming each letter after a tangible object or force extends beyond phonology. It invites an understanding that the script itself was **rooted in the region's worldview** (Haarmann, 1990). This phenomenon resembles, in certain respects, other ancient systems (e.g., Egyptian hieroglyphs) where script and cosmic or territorial references were interlinked. Yet Phoenician stands out for distilling references into a short, standardized set of 22 letters – rather than the hundreds of signs found in Egyptian (Manley, 2012).

1. **Cosmic Markers**: Letters like **Shin** (W) meaning "tooth" and **Ayin** (O) meaning "eye" might evoke a sense of the living body or the cosmic "eye" and "mouth" in local mythology or religious conceptions. Letters referencing fences, doors, or hooks reflect boundaries, thresholds, and structural forms essential to communal living.

2. **Territorial Identity**: The presence of agrarian symbols – oxen, camels, fish – speaks to the Levantine ecosystem. Camels, for instance, enabled trade across deserts, forging a unique identity for Phoenician mariners who traversed land routes to complement their seafaring expertise (Cross, 1980).

In this way, the 22-letter abjad encoded not just the speech sounds but also the **cosmic and territorial** references that shaped Levantine life. Subsequent civilizations that inherited this script might have downplayed or even lost awareness of these connotations, but in Phoenician usage, they remained integral to the script's cultural resonance (Sass, 1988).

2.2.2 "Vocabulary" as Cultural Memory

Because each letter was named after a real object, the entire alphabet functioned like a **catalog** of items crucial to survival and identity. This synergy of letter names and local environment formed a **cultural memory** device. Reciting the alphabet – Aleph, Beth, Gimel, Daleth, etc. – was, in a sense, reciting a short list of the region's key building blocks: its animals, homes, tools, boundaries, water sources, and more (Cross, 1980). Such recitation thus reaffirmed communal knowledge: the very act of learning the letters might have invoked a mental map of the society's environment.

In the long run, as Phoenician traders disseminated their script through Mediterranean trade routes, the practical power of a **22-letter system** overshadowed the specific references. City-states in the Aegean or Italy who adopted these letters primarily valued their utility for transcribing new languages (Greek, Etruscan, Latin), gradually severing the semantic tie to "ox," "house," or "camel." Over time, the script would become more purely alphabetic, focusing on **sound representation** rather than direct references to local fauna or objects (Daniels & Bright, 1996).

A Case for Ontolophemes

Nevertheless, the early phases of **Phoenician** remain a critical stage for comprehending how an **ontology of daily life** could become woven into an alphabet. Indeed, many of the archaic letter names survive in some form across Hebrew, Aramaic, and Arabic scripts, preserving vestiges of these references, even if the modern user rarely perceives their full significance (Haarmann, 1990).

Reflecting on Proto-Sinaitic to Phoenician: The Crucible of Alphabetic Evolution

Bridging the gap from **Proto-Sinaitic** to **Phoenician** reveals a transformation from scattered, experimental consonantal signs to a **standardized abjad** of 22 letters. Proto-Sinaitic is credited with the initial acrophonic insight, gleaning single-consonant signs from pictorial references to local objects and experiences (Sass, 1988). Phoenician honed this tradition, systematically naming each letter after a real-world item and ensuring consistent usage across the Levant and beyond.

The result was more than just a **phonetic tool**; it was a system that **encoded the environment**, reflecting the synergy of commerce, farming, and domestic structures. Whether etched on stelae, scratched onto pottery, or inscribed on official documents, the Phoenician letters conveyed both language and lifestyle. This synergy underpins the notion – explored throughout this work – that alphabets can serve as **ontological** inventories, enumerating a society's core realities.

When the Phoenician script traveled westward, it influenced the **Greek** alphabet, which added vowels to suit Greek phonology. Later, the **Latin** script evolved from Etruscan and Greek variants, eventually spawning the 26 letters of modern English (Sampson, 1985). Yet the seeds of that lineage lie in the modest environment of Levantine city-states, whose scribes and traders recognized the power of a simple, streamlined set of consonants named for the building blocks of their world (Cross, 1980). Recognizing this genealogical arc enriches our understanding of how English orthography – the daily tool of countless writers – can trace its roots back to pragmatic, symbol-laden beginnings in the deserts and coasts of the second millennium BCE.

Concluding Observations

By analyzing the trajectory from **Proto-Sinaitic** to **Phoenician**, we glean the **foundational shift** in alphabetic writing: a transition from largely pictorial references wedded to local environments, to a consolidated abjad that nonetheless preserved a strong conceptual tie to crucial objects like oxen, houses, and camels (Sass, 1988). This shift demonstrates that alphabets need not be purely phonetic codes. On the contrary, each letter might originally reference a real-world object or scenario, forging an **ontology** that merges language with geography, economy, and spirituality (Cross, 1980).

As subsequent chapters examine Greek, Latin, and later English adaptations, the importance of Phoenician remains undeniable. It stands as the **major turning point**, shaping how modern Western alphabets came to exist. By forging a stable set of 22 named consonants, Phoenician scribes carved out a universalizable script, one that could cross linguistic and cultural borders while transmitting vestiges of the environment from which it arose. It is within this continuum that the English alphabet finds its oldest ancestors, even if a casual onlooker today would scarcely suspect that "A" was once an **ox** and "B" a **house**. Yet that is precisely the genealogical truth – and the reason that alphabets, far from neutral arrays of letters, can be viewed as **ontic** or **sacred** reflections of a civilization's lifeways (Daniels & Bright, 1996).

B. Greek Adaptation

The Phoenician script, with its carefully honed 22-letter **abjad** system, revolutionized the recording of Semitic speech and became a linchpin in the Levant's trade and cultural exchange. Yet its historical trajectory did not end along the eastern shores of the Mediterranean: By the 8th century BCE, **Greek communities** in regions such as Euboea and the Aegean islands encountered the Phoenician script – quite possibly through trade or direct contact with Phoenician sailors – and saw in it the potential for creating an **alphabet** suitable for Indo-European Greek (Sampson, 1985; Cross, 1980). The innovations made by these Greek adaptors would decisively shape the course of Western literacy, introducing the **vowel letters** that so deeply influence Latin, Cyrillic, and other scripts derived from Greek in subsequent centuries.

In this section, we explore two major facets of the Greek adaptation of the Phoenician script. First, we examine the **technical and structural changes**, particularly the addition of vowel letters, the dropping or merging of Phoenician graphemes, and the repurposing of certain consonants for new phonemic roles (DeFrancis, 1989; Daniels & Bright, 1996). Second, we investigate the **esoteric retentions** – echoes of the older cosmic or conceptual references embedded in letter names. Though the visual shapes and uses evolved, some intangible vestige of the original ontic significance endured, epitomized in the continuity between Phoenician *Aleph* and Greek *Alpha*, *Beth* and *Beta*, *Gimel* and *Gamma*, and so forth (Cross, 1980).

1. Adaptation of Phoenician Letters

1.1 Vowels Introduced; Shapes Altered

One of the most striking innovations the Greeks introduced to the Phoenician script was the systematic **incor-**

poration of vowels. The original Phoenician abjad was well-suited for Semitic languages, wherein consonantal roots often carry the semantic core, and vowels serve morphological or contextual roles (Sass, 1988). Greek, however, is an Indo-European language whose phonotactics rely more heavily on explicit vowels for both meaning and syllabic structure (Sampson, 1985). Merely having consonant letters would not suffice to represent Greek words, which typically feature **onset-nucleus-coda** syllabic patterns that hinge on vowel clarity.

1.1.1 Repurposing Phoenician Consonants as Vowels

In solving this challenge, Greek scribes ingeniously **repurposed** several Phoenician consonant letters that did not match Greek phonemes and used them instead to mark vowel sounds (Cross, 1980). A prime example is the adaptation of Phoenician **Aleph** (𐤀) – a symbol for a glottal stop in Semitic languages – into Greek **Alpha (A)**, representing the vowel /a/. Another instance is Phoenician **He** (𐤄), which originally indicated a /h/ consonant, becoming Greek **Epsilon (E)** for the vowel /e/ (Sampson, 1985). This process was not always direct or uniform across all Greek dialects, but eventually, standard practices emerged, giving Greek its famed short vowels **(A, E, I, O, Y)** and later additional letters for long vowels or diphthongs **(Ω, H, etc.)** (Daniels & Bright, 1996).

- **Aleph (𐤀) → Alpha (A, α):** From glottal stop to short /a/

- He (𐤄) → Epsilon (E, ε): From /h/ to short /e/

- **Ayin (𐤏) → Omicron (O, o) or Omega (Ω, ω)**, though the details are more complex, as *ayin* functioned differently in various dialects (Sass, 1988).

- **Yod (𐤉) → Iota (I, ι):** /j/ was mapped to /i/ in many Greek dialects

A Case for Ontolophemes

For Greek scribes, this shift seemed intuitive: they needed letters to represent Greek's robust vowel system, and certain "extra" Phoenician consonant letters – unused because Greek lacked those consonants – provided a convenient route (DeFrancis, 1989). Though such repurposing diverged sharply from Phoenician usage, it effectively **completed** the alphabet for Greek linguistic needs, cementing the script's functional viability.

1.1.2 Structural and Aesthetic Alterations

In addition to reassigning consonants to vowels, the **shapes** of many letters underwent modifications to suit local writing practices (Sampson, 1985). Early Greek inscriptions exhibit a variety of local alphabets – known as "epichoric" scripts – across city-states such as **Euboea, Corinth, Athens,** and **Crete** (Jeffery, 1961). Over time, a more standardized Ionic alphabet from **Ionia** in Asia Minor rose to prominence, eventually adopted by Athens in 403 BCE and spreading across the Hellenic world.

- **Aleph → Alpha** saw a transformation from a linear or angular shape reminiscent of a Phoenician ox head into a more triangular form (shaped like an inverted V with a crossbar).

- **Beth → Beta** similarly abandoned some of Phoenician's angular forms for shapes more conducive to writing on stone or pottery with Greek styluses.

- **Gimel → Gamma**, **Daleth → Delta**, and so on, each revealed progressive stylization to match Greek scribal preferences, resulting in distinctive letterforms we now recognize in classical inscriptions (Sass, 1988).

These aesthetic changes also responded to differences in writing surfaces. Greek communities often inscribed on stone stelae, earthenware, or wax tablets, each of which imposed unique constraints on letter shaping (Jeffery, 1961).

Curves, angles, and lines evolved accordingly, further distancing Greek letters from their original Phoenician prototypes.

1.2 Some Phoenician Letters Dropped, Merged, or Repurposed

In the process of **transferring** the Phoenician script to Greek usage, not all original Phoenician letters found a direct function. The Greek language lacked certain consonantal sounds (like the emphatic consonants or the pharyngeal /ʕ/ represented by *ayin*) or used them differently, leading to **dropped** or **merged** letters. Some letters were also **repurposed** to capture Greek-specific phonemes.

1.2.1 Letters Dropped or Merged

- **Samekh (𐤎)**: The Phoenician /s/ eventually overlapped with **Shin (𐤔)** in Greek, and variations of sibilants were collapsed in the earliest Greek alphabets. Over time, Greek ended up with **Sigma (Σ)**, uniting the functions that Phoenician originally split into multiple sibilant letters (Sampson, 1985).

- **Tsade (𐤑)** and **Teth (𐤈)**: Greek had no direct parallels for these **emphatic** or fricative-lateral Semitic consonants, leading to their elimination or merging with simpler /t/ or /s/ letters (Cross, 1980; Sass, 1988).

- **Heth (𐤇)**: Typically a voiceless pharyngeal or velar fricative in Semitic. Greek did not consistently preserve this guttural sound, merging it or discarding it, though some local scripts tried to repurpose it for /h/ (Sampson, 1985).

The resulting Greek system retained only the letters that matched Greek phonemes or could be fruitfully repurposed. This streamlining indicates that the Greek adaptation, while building on Phoenician scaffolding, was always guided by **Greek phonological** needs rather than slavishly mimicking the older script (Daniels & Bright, 1996).

1.2.2 Repurposing and New Letters

As Greek usage grew more standardized, scribes **added** or **transformed** letters to better capture Greek-specific sounds. Notably, letters such as **Phi (Φ), Chi (X),** and **Psi (Ψ)** arose to indicate aspirated or composite consonants (Jeffery, 1961). Some of these transformations are more an outgrowth of local epichoric variation than direct Phoenician input, but the overall process exemplifies how alphabets can be reshaped dramatically when crossing linguistic boundaries:

1. **Upsilon (Y, υ)**: Often traced back to **Waw (Ϙ)** in Phoenician; repurposed in Greek initially as /u/, though eventually representing /y/ in some dialects (Sampson, 1985).

2. **Omega (Ω, ω)**: A later Greek innovation distinguishing long /ɔː/ from the short /o/ already covered by **Omicron (O, o)**. Although not strictly Phoenician, it was integrated into the Greek repertoire, reflecting further script expansion.

Such expansions attested to the **flexibility** of the alphabetic model: once the Greeks grasped the principle of symbol-to-phoneme mapping, it was feasible to add or revise letters for new sounds as needed. The result – **a robust 24-letter Greek alphabet** – would eventually become a blueprint for numerous subsequent scripts, including **Latin**, **Cyrillic**, and various local derivatives across the Mediterranean and Black Sea regions (Daniels & Bright, 1996).

2. Esoteric Retentions

Despite these extensive modifications, the Greek adaptation did not wholly sever the script from its earlier conceptual or symbolic roots. While the functional impetus to represent Greek phonology overshadowed certain aspects of Phoenician cosmic or agrarian references, **echoes** of the older ideas persisted, especially in **letter names** and certain symbolic connotations that survived as cultural lore or classical references (Cross, 1980). In many ways, the Greek script's genealogical tie to Phoenician letters exemplifies how an alphabet can preserve vestigial "ontolophemes" even after crossing major linguistic frontiers (Sass, 1988).

2.1 Even as Shapes Changed, Some Echo of Older Concepts Survived

2.1.1 The Continuity in Letter Names (Alpha, Beta, Gamma, Delta)

One of the clearest markers of **esoteric retention** is the continued usage of letter names derived from Phoenician:

- **Alpha** came from *Aleph*, originally "ox." In Greek, the name no longer signified a bovine animal, but the morphological echo remained.

- **Beta** harks back to *Beth*, signifying "house" in Phoenician. Greek usage preserved the name, although the letter no longer conjured images of domestic architecture for most Greek speakers (Daniels & Bright, 1996).

- **Gamma** and **Delta** follow similar lines, tracing to *Gimel* ("camel") and *Daleth* ("door") respectively, their original references overshadowed yet ironically enshrined in the letter names.

Consequently, an ancient Semitic worldview – oxen, houses, camels, doors – lingered in a Greek vocabulary of letters that had largely shed their direct pictures or agrarian associations (Cross, 1980). It is uncertain whether early Greek scribes recognized or cared about the precise meaning of "Aleph" or "Beth" in Semitic. Likely they deemed it simply the letter's name, which was then adapted to Greek phonotactics (Aleph → Alpha). Nevertheless, the nomenclature's continuity underscores how alphabets can silently bear older cosmic or agrarian linkages forward in time (Sass, 1988).

2.1.2 Ritualistic and Mystical Undercurrents

Although Greek usage mostly repurposed the letters for practical literacy, certain **mystical** or **philosophical** movements glimpsed in these letter forms an **esoteric dimension**. Philosophers and cultic practitioners – particularly in later Hellenic and Hellenistic periods – sometimes attributed symbolic or cosmic significance to the letters themselves (Robinson, 1995). One might note how:

- **Alpha and Omega** in later Christian contexts symbolized the "beginning and the end," as Jesus declares in the Book of Revelation (culturally referencing the first and last letters of the Greek alphabet). The fact that Alpha originally derived from an ox or primal "first letter" in Phoenician abjad underscores a deeper sense of "primordial beginning" that resonates with esoteric usage (Haarmann, 1990).

- Some **Pythagorean** or **Platonic** circles experimented with letter symbolism, though the direct historical evidence for such usage is spottier than we might hope. Even so, alphabetical arrangement sometimes paralleled cosmic or numerological patterns, aligning each letter with a number (Isopsephy in Greece, akin to Gematria in Semitic contexts) (Grafton & Most, 2003).

These spiritual or philosophical expansions of letter significance highlight the persistence of a broader **conceptu-**

al or **ontological** domain within the alphabet, even if the everyday scribe regarded letters as purely phonetic tools (Daniels & Bright, 1996).

2.2 Letter Shapes as Cultural Memory
2.2.1 Transformations in Early Greek Epichoric Scripts

While the **epichoric variations** in letter shapes (e.g., how Euboean Beta vs. Ionian Beta looked) reflect local tastes, one might also see them as partial carriers of the older pictorial references. For instance, a letter form might still hint at an angle or loop reminiscent of the Phoenician original, though now stylized or inverted. Such half-faded echoes remind us that letters seldom transform all at once; their shapes gradually morph over centuries, storing fragments of past visual identities (Jeffery, 1961). If a letter originally depicted a "house plan," the Greek transformation might keep certain strokes that inadvertently recall that structure – albeit unrecognizable to most observers.

2.2.2 The Inheritance of "Glyphic Memory"

In the sense of **ontolophemes**, Greek glyphs can still harbor what we might term a "glyphic memory" of older references (Haarmann, 1990). Even if Greek scribes did not consciously see Beta as a "house," the letter's morphological lineage ensures that the shape, name, and genealogical "DNA" of the letter remains anchored in that concept. As the script disseminated, each new generation inherited a letter set where traces of oxen, doors, and camels lingered. Over time, such associations receded into the realm of esoteric knowledge or philological curiosity, overshadowed by the letter's day-to-day function in representing Greek phonemes.

Connecting Greek Adaptation to Broader Alphabetic Evolution

3.1 Paving the Way for Latin

The **Greek adaptation** proved pivotal for the subsequent development of the **Latin** alphabet, which emerged via the Etruscans who inhabited northern Italy. The Etruscans borrowed a Western Greek variant of the script (commonly from Cumae in southern Italy) and adapted it for Etruscan phonology. Then, as Rome's influence spread, the Latin alphabet took shape, eventually overshadowing Etruscan usage (Sampson, 1985). This genealogical chain underscores how the decisions made by early Greek scribes – particularly the introduction of vowel letters – rippled outward, shaping the eventual scripts of Western Europe (Crystal, 2003).

3.2 Bridging Phoenician Ontology to European Letters

Through Greek adaptation, the concept of alphabets as "ontic inventories" extended its lifespan. By the time these letters reached Rome and beyond, few recognized that "A" and "B" once referenced an ox and a house in a Levantine society (Cross, 1980). Nonetheless, the underlying genealogical truth stands: a **cosmic** or **territorial** vocabulary from Semitic languages had been partially transplanted into Greek letter names, shaping the skeleton of Western scripts. The esoteric dimension became more implicit, surviving in letters' naming traditions and morphological skeletons, rather than explicit references to livestock or architecture (DeFrancis, 1989).

Conclusions on Greek Adaptation

In sum, the Greek adaptation of Phoenician letters represents a **fascinating fusion** of pragmatic linguistic reform and subtle cultural inheritance:

1. **Phonetic Reform**: By adding vowels and dropping or merging certain Phoenician consonants, Greek scribes created a script tailored to Indo-European phonology. This crucial innovation rippled through the classical world, influencing literacy in regions that fell under Greek cultural sway (Daniels & Bright, 1996).

2. **Shape and Form Evolutions**: Greek letter shapes diverged from Phoenician prototypes in response to local scribal practices, available writing materials, and aesthetic norms. Regional variations gradually converged into a more standardized alphabet by the mid to late 5th century BCE (Jeffery, 1961).

3. **Esoteric Continuity**: Despite significant transformations, the Greek alphabet retained letter names – Alpha, Beta, Gamma, Delta – directly echoing Semitic references to an "ox," "house," "camel," and "door." Over centuries, these references, though no longer recognized by the average user, maintained a symbolic chain of inheritance, linking Greek literacy to Levantine cultural concepts (Cross, 1980).

4. **Cultural and Mystical Resonances**: While the prime impetus for adopting Phoenician letters was probably commercial and administrative efficiency, a faint mystic or esoteric element persisted through letter names, potential numerological practices (like isopsephy), and eventual theological usage (e.g., Alpha and Omega symbolism) (Grafton & Most, 2003; Haarmann, 1990).

The Greek adaptation serves as an **exemplar** of how alphabets evolve across linguistic boundaries, blending local needs with borrowed letterstock. In the continuum from Phoenician to Greek, we see a partial retention of the archaic references that once mapped daily life – oxen, houses, fish, water – onto script. This bridging testifies to the **power of alphabets** not merely as phonetic codes but as palimpsests of

A Case for Ontolophemes

cultural memory. When we consider the eventual bequest of Greek letters to Latin, and thus to English and other European tongues, the genealogical lines stand out: behind each modern letter lurks an ancient tradition, shaped and reshaped by the adaptive interplay of environment, phonology, and intangible references to an older cosmic or territorial worldview (Sass, 1988).

In the chapters that follow, we will observe how the **Latin** appropriation further modifies these Greek forms, culminating in the familiar 26-letter exoteric system used by millions worldwide. Yet the Greek moment remains vital: it crystallized the concept of a truly **alphabetic** script, forging a robust synergy between consonants and vowels, and planting seeds of tradition that would bloom in diverse literary and scholarly cultures for millennia to come (Daniels & Bright, 1996; Sampson, 1985).

Icosikaihexagon and Icosihenagon

C. Latin and the Emergence of 26 Letters

The Roman alphabet's ascendance is integral to understanding how **English orthography** evolved from a roughly 22-letter Semitic-Greek inheritance into a **26-letter system**. Latin script, widely known as the foundation of writing throughout Western Europe, took shape from local adaptations of Etruscan and Greek letter forms, then underwent centuries of incremental retooling to address the phonological needs of Latin and other languages that later co-opted the script (Sampson, 1985). In this section, we investigate how Latin inherited the basics of an alphabetic framework from Etruscan-Greek origins and how that basic letter set eventually morphed – through splitting, duplication, and even partial re-creation – into a sprawling repertoire of 26 letters. Ultimately, we see that this expansion did not yield new "fundamental objects," but rather a **simulacrum** wherein additional letters masked the relatively small store of ancestral concepts at the script's root (Daniels & Bright, 1996).

1. The Roman Alphabet

1.1 Latin's Inheritance from Etruscan and Greek

Latin emerged in the west-central region of the Italian Peninsula, in contact with a variety of neighboring languages – most notably **Etruscan**, a non-Indo-European tongue spoken by the Etruscans in northern Italy (Bonfante, 1990). By the mid-first millennium BCE, Etruscans themselves had borrowed or adapted a **Western Greek** alphabetic variant from Greek colonies (such as those in **Cumae**, near modern-day Naples). Consequently, the letter shapes used by Etruscan scribes bore strong resemblance to archaic Greek forms (Jeffery, 1961). Although Etruscan phonology diverged from Greek, it retained the general principle of a consonant-plus-vowel script, albeit discarding or altering letters that lacked equivalents in Etruscan speech (Sampson, 1985).

In time, the Latin-speaking communities in the region of **Latium** (including Rome) appropriated this Etruscan adaptation, molding it to fit **Latin** phonology. Early Latin inscriptions reveal an evolving letter set: many Greek letters appear in shapes reminiscent of Ionian or Cumaean forms, though with local stylizations. As Roman power expanded, so did the script's reach, standardizing forms and phasing out ephemeral variants. By approximately the 3rd century BCE, the essential **Roman alphabet** took shape, featuring around 21 letters (Crystal, 2003). Notably, certain Greek letters – for instance, **K, Z,** and **Y** – were initially dropped or marginally retained, because early Latin did not require them for native words. Later, some were reintroduced for technical or loanword purposes (e.g., "Z" for Greek loans, "Y" from Greek upsilon), illustrating that the Roman alphabet was never static but a living system undergoing repeated refinement (Sampson, 1985).

1.1.1 Early Forms and the Core Letter Set

The earliest standardized or near-standardized Roman alphabet likely included:

1. A, B, C, D, E, F, G, H, I, K, L, M, N, O, P, Q, R, S, T, V, X.

- **C** was used for both /k/ and /g/ sounds in the earliest inscriptions, though the letter **G** was eventually introduced by modifying "C" with an added stroke or tail, allowing the script to differentiate /g/ from /k/ (Daniels & Bright, 1996).

- **K** was largely reserved for a few archaic words or abbreviations and gradually diminished in usage, replaced by "C" in most positions representing /k/.

- **Q** typically preceded "V" to represent the labialized velar /kw/ (Sampson, 1985).
- **X** signified /ks/, absorbing what in Greek had sometimes been spelled with chi (X) or xi (Ξ).

This earliest Roman repertoire thus reflected practical solutions for recording Latin phonemes rather than a direct replication of any Greek subset. Each letter's shape or name had passed through a chain of transformations from Phoenician to Greek to Etruscan before arriving in Roman usage (Cross, 1980). Unsurprisingly, the original references to "ox," "house," "camel," and so forth were barely known to Roman scribes, overshadowed by purely phonetic concerns.

1.2 Splitting of Single Letters into Multiple Forms (I/J, U/V/W, G from C, etc.)

Over centuries, the Roman script underwent **splitting** phenomena, in which a single letter originally served multiple phonemes but eventually bifurcated to capture separate sounds. Several major splits stand out (Daniels & Bright, 1996):

1. I/J:
   - In classical Latin, the letter **I** denoted both the vowel /i/ and the consonantal glide /j/. For instance, "Iulius" (Julius) in classical orthography might spell both /i/ and /j/ with "I."
   - By medieval and early modern times, scribes began distinguishing the consonantal form with a tail or hook, evolving into **J** for /dʒ/ or /j/ and maintaining **I** for the vowel /i/ (Crystal, 2003).
   - This differentiation spread unevenly across Europe, but by the Renaissance, "I" and "J" were recognized as distinct letters in many contexts, culminating in modern usage where

English "J" represents /dʒ/ (e.g., "joy," "judge").

2. U/V/W:
   - Latin recognized only one symbol **V** for both the vowel /u/ and the consonant /v/, as evidenced by classical spellings like "AVGVSTVS" (Augustus).
   - With time, medieval scribes began curving "V" into **U** to denote the vowel, while retaining a pointed "V" form for the consonant /v/.
   - When Germanic-speaking regions adopted Latin script to record their own languages, they needed to represent the **/w/** sound, absent in classical Latin. They doubled "U" or "V," forming **W** (initially "double-U") for Germanic words. Thus, "U," "V," and "W" all trace back to the same Phoenician glyph (*Waw* ᚤ), but diversified in Latin script usage (Sampson, 1985).

3. G from C:
   - As noted, "C" once covered both /k/ and /g/ in archaic Latin. Eventually, scribes introduced a variant with a small added stroke: **G**, specifically for /g/.
   - The resulting distinction allowed Latin to represent words like "Gallia" (Gaul) and "Callidus" (clever) with separate letters, clarifying the phonemic difference (Sampson, 1985).

These splits underscore that the Roman alphabet responded dynamically to new phonological pressures. Each newly introduced letter might appear to expand the script's inventory but did not necessarily add a novel conceptual lineage. Rather, these expansions mirrored the functional demands of representing distinct sounds in Latin (Crystal, 2003). Over centuries, new languages borrowing the Roman alphabet – like Old English, French, Spanish, or German – similarly sought ways to accommodate or modify these letters, driving further expansions like diacritical marks (á, ü, ñ, etc.), though English remained relatively diacritic-free (Sampson, 1985).

2. Duplication and Expansion

By the time the Roman Empire had spread across Europe, the script's usage proliferated, eventually giving rise to the **Latin alphabet** as the common foundation for diverse vernaculars (Crystal, 2003). Over generations, even more letters rejoined the repertoire – **Y** and **Z**, for instance, re-imported from Greek in the 1st century BCE to transcribe Greek loanwords. Meanwhile, Middle and Early Modern English scribes refined or introduced **J, U,** and **W** as distinct symbols. These expansions collectively pushed the Roman alphabet from around 21 or 22 letters to a robust total of **26** in modern English (Sampson, 1985).

2.1 Why 22 Letters Became 26 in English

Although ancient Latin might have had 21–23 letters in certain phases, by Late Antiquity and the early Middle Ages, a set of around **23 or 24** letters was standard in various scribal traditions (Daniels & Bright, 1996). The path to **26** specifically in English hinged on key developments:

1. Insertion of "J":
    - As Medieval Latin script usage diversified, scribes distinguished consonantal /j/ from vowel /i/ by appending a tail, especially at word-initial positions. This practice eventually crystallized into the letter "J" (Crystal, 2003).

A Case for Ontolophemes

- By the time of the printing press, "J" was broadly accepted in English for /dʒ/, as in "joy," "judge," "James."

2. Separation of "U" and "V":

   - The pointed "V" shape served for both the vowel /u/ and the consonant /v/ in classical Latin inscriptions. In medieval script, scribes began using a rounded form "u" in the middle of words and "v" at word boundaries (Sampson, 1985).

   - By Early Modern English, the two shapes were recognized as distinct letters with separate phonetic functions (/u/ vs. /v/). This distinction was codified in printed texts of the 16th and 17th centuries.

3. Emergence of "W":

   - Germanic languages needed a symbol for /w/. English inherited "uu" or "double-u" to denote that sound, eventually rendered as "w."

   - Despite forming a single phoneme, "W" came to be counted as a separate letter, raising the total count in the alphabet.

4. Reintroduction of "Y" and "Z":

   - The letters "Y" (from Greek upsilon) and "Z" (from Greek zeta) appear in classical Latin but were removed in older periods for lack of usage in native words. They re-entered for writing Greek loanwords or transliterating foreign names (Sampson, 1985). English usage inherited them, thereby boosting the total letter count.

By the completion of these processes – most vividly visible in Renaissance English printing – the alphabet displayed **26 discrete letters**: A, B, C, D, E, F, G, H, I, J, K, L, M, N, O, P, Q, R, S, T, U, V, W, X, Y, Z (Crystal, 2003). This final inventory defined the "modern English alphabet" as recognized in classrooms today.

2.1.1 Historical "Accidents" and Orthographic Forces

This expansion from 22 to 26 was not the result of a single reform or decree but a gradual series of orthographic "accidents" or local scribal conventions that coalesced over time (Sampson, 1985). Printing technology, which became influential in Europe from the mid-15th century onward (Johann Gutenberg's press), standardized many of these changes. Printers needed consistent typefaces for each letter, codifying the separation between I/J and U/V/W in their fonts, thus institutionalizing these earlier scribal distinctions (Crystal, 2003).

Moreover, the impetus behind each addition was **phonetic clarity** or **foreign loanword assimilation**, not any desire to resurrect or expand the script's conceptual foundation (Daniels & Bright, 1996). This means that while the Roman alphabet outwardly appeared "larger," the older ontic or cosmic associations from Phoenician and Greek times remained essentially buried. Each new letter was genealogically linked to a smaller set of original Phoenician glyphs – like **Waw** (𐤅) spawning U, V, W, Y, or **Yod** (𐤉) spawning I/J. Even the re-importation of "Z" or "Y" from Greek references the same remote origins in Phoenician *Zayin* ("weapon?") or *Waw* ("hook/peg?") (Sass, 1988).

2.2 Creation of a "Simulacrum": More Letters, but Not More Fundamental Objects

By the time English orthography settled into a 26-letter system, it is tempting to view these letters as 26 **fully dis-**

A Case for Ontolophemes

tinct symbolic units. Yet from the vantage of genealogical or ontic significance, many of these expansions represent **duplications** or **branches** of the same underlying concept. The outcome is what we might call a "**simulacrum**": a superficially enlarged set of graphemes that does not actually increase the **conceptual base** from the Phoenician or proto-Sinaitic scripts (Cross, 1980).

1. **U, V, W, Y** share the same Phoenician root: **Waw** (𐤅), typically meaning "hook" or "peg." The fact that they appear as four separate letters in modern English – each with its own shape and phonetic usage – does not alter their genealogical unity (Sampson, 1985).

2. **I, J** both descend from **Yod** (𐤉), referencing "hand/arm," though English speakers rarely link these letters to manual limbs.

3. **C, G** trace back to **Gimel** (𐤂) ("camel" in Phoenician), with "G" splitting off from an original "C" shape to differentiate /g/ from /k/ (Daniels & Bright, 1996).

Thus, while the exoteric surface of the English alphabet shows 26 letters, the **esoteric** or genealogical depth remains smaller, closer to the **21 or 22** fundamental concepts from Phoenician. This discrepancy reflects centuries of orthographic improvisation aimed at capturing new phonetic distinctions or borrowed words, rather than introducing fresh cosmic or agrarian referents. In other words, the phonetic demands of Latin and its daughter languages overshadowed the original symbolic dimension, thereby forging an **increased letter count** without a commensurate expansion in conceptual foundations (DeFrancis, 1989).

2.2.1 Illustrating the Simulacrum

The concept of a **simulacrum** highlights that modern English, with 26 letters, does not directly map onto 26 distinct archaic "objects" or "forces," but rather a smaller set of conceptual "seeds" (Sass, 1988). A letter like **U** and a letter like **V** might appear fully distinct in daily usage, yet genealogically they converge on a single origin. Thus, the icosikaihexagon (26 sides) is an outward shell that disguises the icosihenagon or proto-ontology of around 21–22 sides. The resulting tension helps explain why, from an esoteric or historical-linguistic perspective, the modern alphabet can be considered both larger (for practical phonetic coverage) and smaller (by conceptual measure) than it appears (Haarmann, 1990).

2.2.2 Cultural Implications

From a purely **functional** viewpoint, the expansion to 26 letters is a boon for literacy: it allows English to represent a wide array of phonemes (albeit imperfectly, given English spelling's complexities). However, the original "iconic" or "ontic" references remain lost in a labyrinth of expansions, merges, splits, and reintroductions. That is why few modern Anglophones realize that "G" is the scion of "C," which traces to a Phoenician camel, or that "W" and "U" share a link to the same ancient "hook" (Daniels & Bright, 1996). Modern usage frames each letter as an independent entity, ignoring genealogical overlap.

This phenomenon underscores a broader principle: alphabets, though initially derived from **ontological** or **pictographic** contexts, can evolve in such ways that the conceptual or cosmic anchors fade behind a purely orthographic or phonetic function (Crystal, 2003). The Roman and, eventually, English expansions demonstrate how new letters can accrue to solve immediate linguistic tasks – differentiating /v/ from /u/, or /dʒ/ from /i/ – without any impetus to maintain or evolve the original symbolic universe. The result is a script outwardly "larger" but not necessarily "deeper" in the esoteric sense (DeFrancis, 1989).

A Case for Ontolophemes

Concluding Observations on the Latin Emergence of 26 Letters

Through Latin's inheritance of Etruscan-Greek letter forms, the West found a script that would become **exceedingly adaptable**, ultimately shaping literacy across Europe and many parts of the globe (Sampson, 1985). The Roman Empire's influence, followed by medieval and Renaissance scribal traditions, stabilized and enriched the script, ensuring that it could accommodate the phonological complexities of Latin, then those of the Germanic, Romance, and other languages that used Latin script as a basis (Crystal, 2003). This entailed **splitting** once-unified letters and **expanding** the overall inventory by reintroducing Greek-based symbols or re-purposing single letters into multiple roles.

However, this wave of expansions – resulting in the eventual **26-letter** English alphabet – did not represent an infusion of new conceptual or cosmic references. Rather, it was an **accumulation of variants** derived from a smaller set of ancestral Phoenician glyphs. In that sense, the final exoteric shape of English orthography, with its distinct letters "I," "J," "U," "V," "W," "Y," etc., can be seen as a **simulacrum**: an outwardly multiplied structure concealing a deeper genealogical unity (Cross, 1980; Sass, 1988). Each letter's genealogical or esoteric dimension remains overshadowed, having long since been eclipsed by orthographic pragmatism and the demands of printing standardization (Crystal, 2003).

Therefore, understanding how **Latin** shaped the emergence of these 26 letters invites us to question the very nature of alphabetical proliferation: is the modern English alphabet truly larger than its Phoenician ancestor in any conceptual sense, or is it simply an elaboration on older foundations? Most evidence suggests the latter. While functionally more flexible and attuned to new phonemic distinctions, English orthography does not rest on a richer conceptual lattice;

rather, it rests on historical duplications rooted in a modest inventory of ancient ontic seeds (Daniels & Bright, 1996). Recognizing this duality – between the exoteric expansions and the esoteric unities – sheds light on how alphabets evolve and how the deeper mythic or cosmic references can be easily obscured in the service of practical writing.

IV. THE 21 FUNDAMENTAL OBJECTS (ICOSIHENAGON)

A. Master List of Core Ontic Units

In the labyrinthine genealogy of alphabets – stretching from Proto-Sinaitic pictographs through Phoenician abjads, Greek vowels, and ultimately to the English script – one discovers a remarkable consistency of underlying **conceptual roots**. Where modern alphabets often display more numerous letters, replete with splits and duplications, their ultimate ancestry in Semitic sources reduces to a more compact inventory of objects and ideas. These items, typically estimated at around **21**, can be considered the **core "ontic units"** or **ontolophemes** that once served as a living record of Bronze Age and Iron Age Levantine life (Cross, 1980; Sass, 1988). Their presence suggests that each letter was originally connected to a material or spiritual reference, and that the eventual emergence of 26 letters in English – a so-called icosikaihexagon – rests on fewer fundamental pillars, best symbolized by an **icosihenagon** of conceptual roots.

Below, we present a **master list** of these conceptual seeds. Although some debate exists regarding the precise meaning of certain Phoenician or Proto-Sinaitic glyphs, the general consensus converges around the following core references. They include agrarian and pastoral items, domestic structures, key body parts, and occasional mystical or ambiguous images. Each served not just as a phonetic marker but as an *ontic index* – a window into the worldview of the peoples who first harnessed pictorial signs for the creation of alphabets (Daniels & Bright, 1996; Haarmann, 1990).

A Case for Ontolophemes

1. Ox

   - **Name Origin**: Phoenician *Aleph* (𐤀), signifying "ox." Proto-Sinaitic inscriptions often depict a stylized ox head.

   - **Symbolic/Practical Meaning**: Oxen were indispensable in agrarian societies for plowing and transport, representing strength and fertility. Over time, *Aleph* became Greek **Alpha (A)**, which then evolved into the Latin **A**.

   - **Modern Duplication**: Greek "A" and Latin "A" remain single forms, but the root "ox" meaning eventually faded from everyday usage, retained only in genealogical studies (Cross, 1980).

2. House

   - **Name Origin**: Phoenician *Beth* (𐤁), originally a schematic depiction of a house's floor plan.

   - **Symbolic/Practical Meaning**: In Bronze Age communities, the "house" was a vital symbol of domestic life and security.

   - **Modern Duplication**: Greek **Beta (B)** and Latin **B** preserve the name, but no additional letters were derived from this root in English, so duplication is minimal here (Daniels & Bright, 1996).

3. Camel

   - **Name Origin**: Phoenician *Gimel* (𐤂). The letter name references a "camel," crucial for trade routes crossing deserts.

   - **Symbolic/Practical Meaning**: The camel was a prime beast of burden, enabling commercial and cultural exchange in the Levant.

- **Modern Duplication**: **G** in Latin script descends from a modified "C," both of which trace back to *Gimel*. Thus, **C** and **G** share one root, highlighting how a single concept – "camel" – came to spawn two distinct letters in modern alphabets (Sass, 1988).

4. Door

- **Name Origin**: Phoenician *Daleth* (◁), referencing a door or gateway.

- **Symbolic/Practical Meaning**: Doors mark thresholds between public and private spaces, an essential architectural feature.

- **Modern Duplication**: Greek **Delta (Δ)** and Latin **D** each reflect the door concept, but no further letters sprung from this root in English (Cross, 1980).

5. Window/Breath

- **Name Origin**: Phoenician *He* (♀), sometimes glossed as "window" or "breath." Semitic roots occasionally connect it to an exclamatory or aspirated sound.

- **Symbolic/Practical Meaning**: The concept of an opening – be it a literal window or a channel for breath – has resonance in many cultural contexts, often linked to air flow or light.

- **Modern Duplication**: Greek repurposed it to represent the vowel /e/ (Epsilon), diverging from the aspirate meaning. No direct duplication in English letters emerges here, though "E" stands genealogically behind multiple vowel functions (Sampson, 1985).

6. Hook/Peg

- **Name Origin**: Phoenician *Waw* (Y), typically described as a "hook" or "peg."

- **Symbolic/Practical Meaning**: Tents and simple structures in the Levant required pegs or hooks for stability, essential in nomadic or semi-nomadic communities.

- **Modern Duplication**: The single *Waw* led to **U, V, W, Y** in modern English – demonstrating a striking case of duplication. All four letters share the same conceptual lineage, signifying a "hook" or "peg" at the root (Crystal, 2003).

7. Fence

- **Name Origin**: Phoenician *Heth* (目), hypothesized as "fence" or "enclosure."

- **Symbolic/Practical Meaning**: Fences demarcated territory, safeguarding crops and livestock. They symbolized ownership and boundary.

- **Modern Duplication**: Greek scripts often merged or dropped the pharyngeal connotation of this letter, and it did not survive distinctly in Latin. Thus, it is overshadowed, though it remains in the genealogical record (Sass, 1988).

8. Hand/Arm

- **Name Origin**: Phoenician *Yod* (Z), referencing a "hand" or "arm."

- **Symbolic/Practical Meaning**: The human hand embodies action, craft, and manipulation of the environment.

- **Modern Duplication**: **I** and **J** both trace to *Yod*, revealing duplication as scribes distinguished vowel /i/ from consonantal /j/ (/dʒ/ in English). The conceptual reference to "hand" or "arm" remains only in historical-linguistic memory (Cross, 1980).

9. Palm (of the Hand)

- **Name Origin**: Phoenician *Kaph* (𐤊), meaning the "palm."

- **Symbolic/Practical Meaning**: An extension of the hand theme, the palm underscores manual dexterity and the capacity to grip or hold.

- **Modern Duplication**: Greek **Kappa (K)** led to Latin **K** (eventually limited usage) and also bled into the function of **C** in some contexts. Over time, the conceptual link to a "palm" was all but lost (Sampson, 1985).

10. Goad (Cattle Prod)

- **Name Origin**: Phoenician *Lamedh* (𐤋), sometimes translated "goad" or "cattle prod."

- **Symbolic/Practical Meaning**: A tool for herding or directing livestock, reinforcing the pastoral reality of many Levantine societies.

- **Modern Duplication**: Greek **Lambda (Λ)** became Latin **L**, with minimal branching in English. The reference to a "goad" is a faint echo of agrarian culture (Haarmann, 1990).

11. Water

- **Name Origin**: Phoenician *Mem* (𐤌), visually depicted as wavy lines.

- **Symbolic/Practical Meaning**: Water is critical for sustenance, irrigation, and ritual. In many traditions, it also symbolizes chaos or life's primordial element.

- **Modern Duplication**: Greek **Mu (M)** → Latin **M**. No further duplication emerged in English from this root, although "M" remains crucial in referencing /m/ (Daniels & Bright, 1996).

A Case for Ontolophemes

12. Fish

   - **Name Origin**: Phoenician *Nun* (𐤍), literally "fish."
   - **Symbolic/Practical Meaning**: Fish served as a vital food resource, denoting livelihood in maritime or riverine regions.
   - **Modern Duplication**: Greek **Nu (N)** → Latin **N**. The letter name's original aquatic link disappeared in mainstream usage, overshadowed by purely phonetic concerns (Sass, 1988).

13. Eye

   - **Name Origin**: Phoenician *Ayin* (𐤏), "eye." Early pictographs might have approximated an eye shape.
   - **Symbolic/Practical Meaning**: Vision represents perception, awareness, and, in some cultures, an esoteric "window to the soul."
   - **Modern Duplication**: Ayin originally indicated a voiced pharyngeal constriction in Semitic – absent in Greek and Latin, so it was often reused as a vowel letter (e.g., **Omicron**, **Omega**). Thus, duplication is partial, with the original concept overshadowed (Cross, 1980).

14. Mouth

   - **Name Origin**: Phoenician *Pe* (𐤐), referencing the mouth.
   - **Symbolic/Practical Meaning**: The mouth is central to speech and nourishment, bridging communication and sustenance.
   - **Modern Duplication**: Greek **Pi (Π)** → Latin **P**. No secondary splits in English, though the link to

"mouth" has faded from everyday consciousness (Sampson, 1985).

15. Monkey/Back of Head/Needle's Eye

- **Name Origin**: Phoenician *Qoph* (𐤒). A contested letter, sometimes interpreted as referencing a monkey, the back of the head, or a hole resembling a needle's eye.

- **Symbolic/Practical Meaning**: Though ambiguous, *Qoph* underscores how lesser-documented or rarer concepts could enter the script. Monkeys or apes might have been exotic symbols, while "back of head" or "needle's eye" references carry varied connotations in lexicon or folklore (Sass, 1988).

- **Modern Duplication**: Greek borrowed it in forms corresponding to **Koppa** (Ϙ), later dropped or repurposed. Latin kept **Q** as a /kw/ marker in combination with **U**, leading to expansions in English, though the concept of a "monkey" or "needle's eye" has long vanished (Cross, 1980).

16. Head

- **Name Origin**: Phoenician *Resh* (𐤓), meaning "head."

- **Symbolic/Practical Meaning**: The head often symbolizes leadership or the topmost element.

- **Modern Duplication**: Greek **Rho (Ρ)** → Latin **R**. No additional branching in English, though the original "head" significance is almost entirely lost (Daniels & Bright, 1996).

17. Tooth

- **Name Origin**: Phoenician *Shin* (𐤔), "tooth." In early pictographs, it may have shown multiple vertical lines representing teeth.

- **Symbolic/Practical Meaning**: Teeth highlight consumption, defense, and the primal aspect of sustenance.

- **Modern Duplication**: Greek **Sigma** or **San** occasionally trace back to similar sibilant roots. Latin **S** is the direct descendant. Overlaps exist with **Samekh** or other sibilants, leading to partial merges (Sampson, 1985).

18. Mark/Cross

- **Name Origin**: Phoenician *Taw* (✝), signifying a "mark" or "cross."

- **Symbolic/Practical Meaning**: A simplified cross or plus sign was an indicator of boundary, ownership, or personal signature (for those illiterate in standard scripts).

- **Modern Duplication**: Greek **Tau (T)** → Latin **T**. Unsplit in English, though far removed from the idea of a "mark" or "signature" today (Cross, 1980).

19. Spine/Backbone

- **Name Origin**: Commonly linked to Phoenician *Samekh* (𐤎), though interpretations vary ("support," "fish spine," or "peg").

- **Symbolic/Practical Meaning**: A "spine" or "backbone" can represent structural integrity.

- **Modern Duplication**: Some scholars see Greek **Xi (Ξ)** as derivative. In Latin usage, **X** stands for /ks/, overshadowing the original concept (Sass, 1988).

20. Sword/Weapon

- **Name Origin**: Phoenician *Zayin* (𐤆), possibly "weapon," "sword," or "spear."

- **Symbolic/Practical Meaning**: Denoting martial power or protection in a region where warfare and defense were routine concerns.

- **Modern Duplication**: Greek **Zeta (Z)** → Latin **Z**, often reintroduced for loanwords. Rare usage in early Latin but revived later. Any reference to an actual weapon is lost in mainstream orthography (Crystal, 2003).

21. (Possible Additions or Variations)

A handful of other letters or concepts appear in earlier scripts but remain contested or ephemeral. Scholars sometimes mention **Teth (⊕)** or **Sadhe (ኘ)** for specific Semitic sounds representing unique objects. Whether these become part of the standard 21 or 22 depends on the classification used. Nonetheless, each letter's name or shape alludes to a physical or conceptual domain once integral to the environment (Sass, 1988).

Where Duplication Originally Came From

A striking feature of these **21** (or **22**) ontic units is that multiple **modern letters** often share the same deep origin. The expansions in Greek, Etruscan, Latin, and subsequently English, caused some single Phoenician glyphs to branch into two, three, or four **exoteric** letters (Daniels & Bright, 1996). For instance:

- **Waw (Y)** → **U, V, W, Y** in English

- Yod (Z) → I, J

- Gimel (𐤂) → C, G

- **Aleph (𐤀)** → **Alpha (A)** → **A** (but reinterpreted as a vowel in Greek)

A Case for Ontolophemes

This branching emerges not from any newly introduced conceptual domain, but from orthographic and phonetic adjustments – splitting letters to capture different sounds in new languages, or reimporting Greek letters for foreign loanwords (Sampson, 1985). Hence, **modern alphabets** may appear to possess more letters than their ancestors did, but genealogically, they reference the **same** original inventory of objects and cosmic or daily-life forces.

Significance of the Icosihenagon

By collecting these 21 concepts, we arrive at the **icosihenagon**, a metaphorical polygon of 21 sides – each side representing a **fundamental object** or notion. While the exact list may vary slightly among scholars (some maintain 22, others debate the meaning of certain letters), the crux remains: underneath the outward 26 letters of English lies a condensed conceptual blueprint reflecting the Bronze Age Levant, replete with references to pastoral, domestic, and bodily realities (Cross, 1980). The **"exoteric"** English alphabet, in other words, is but an outward shell for these archaic seeds.

In discussing these items as "**ontic units**," we underscore their once-living status in everyday activities – herding, traveling, building houses, ensuring water supply, and possibly engaging in warfare or trade. Not merely abstract shapes, each letter captured a slice of that environment. Over millennia, as alphabets migrated through Greek, Etruscan, Latin, and into modern languages, the pictures and references blurred or disappeared, yielding purely phonetic usage while retaining genealogical shadows of the older worldview (Haarmann, 1990).

Concluding Reflections

The **master list of core ontic units** – ox, house, camel, door, and so on – serves as a crucial lens for comprehending how alphabets began as **ontological** mappings, not solely phonetic transcriptions. Whether referencing the earliest Proto-Sinaitic carvings or the standardization of Phoenician letters, each entry in this list underscores how basic survival, domestic space, social constructs, and even spiritual concepts shaped the earliest writing systems. The presence of duplication in the modern age reveals a dynamic interplay: alphabets expanded in letter count for phonetic necessity, yet they rarely introduced new conceptual roots.

Hence, in discussing alphabets as **sacred geometries** or ontic frameworks, we rediscover the synergy between script and **life-world**. Far from being trivial squiggles, these letters – once recognized as referencing oxen, fish, fences, or pegs – remind us that writing systems emerged in direct dialogue with human labor, ecology, and spirituality (Daniels & Bright, 1996; Sass, 1988). Even in the modern era, while few recall that "A" signifies an ox and "B" a house, the genealogical trace remains intact for those willing to journey back through the millennia. And that journey, symbolized by the **icosihenagon**, reveals an alphabet that is more than 26 letters on a page: it is the inherited lattice of human concepts, shaped by time, trade, and cultural imagination.

A Case for Ontolophemes

B. Symbolic and Mythic Implications

1. Cultural Reflection

The script-objects we have identified – ranging from the **Ox** (Aleph) to the **Door** (Daleth), and from the **Fish** (Nun) to the **House** (Beth) – are not mere phonetic placeholders in a historical timeline. Rather, they encapsulate deep cultural resonances linked to agrarian and pastoral life in the Bronze Age Levant (Cross, 1980). By examining these signified objects from an anthropological and mythic standpoint, we unearth a **material-spiritual synergy** that reveals how each letter once mirrored the values, survival imperatives, and sacred dimensions of the communities that birthed them (Sass, 1988). In this section, we explore how these signs served as **cultural reflections**, embedding a worldview that melded the practical and the esoteric – ultimately influencing the shape and content of the alphabets that have come down to us.

The Agrarian and Pastoral Milieu

In the Levantine environment of the second millennium BCE, life centered on **agriculture, herding, and small-scale trade**. Communities cultivated cereals like wheat and barley, raised goats, sheep, oxen, and occasionally relied on camels for transport. The region's climate, punctuated by hot summers and modest rainy seasons, reinforced an acute awareness of resources such as **water** (Mem) – a substance so crucial that it came to symbolize both chaos and the life-giving force in Semitic cosmologies (DeFrancis, 1989). Against this backdrop, the letters that eventually formed the Phoenician abjad (and, by extension, our modern alphabets) not only listed out the building blocks of day-to-day subsistence – fish, oxen, houses – but also hinted at more **mythic or spiritual** dimensions.

Icosikaihexagon and Icosihenagon

1. Ox (Aleph)

    - **Material Role**: The ox was indispensable for plowing and hauling, signifying physical power and the "engine" of early agriculture.

    - **Mythic Connotation**: In many ancient cultures, bull or ox imagery conveyed fertility and generative energy (Haarmann, 1990). The Canaanite god Baal was sometimes depicted with bovine attributes, underscoring the animal's sacred presence in ritual contexts.

2. House (Beth)

    - **Material Role**: A house was not merely a shelter but also a locus of family life, inheritance, and social identity (Cross, 1980).

    - **Mythic Connotation**: Houses, especially in early Levantine societies, often contained domestic altars or symbols for ancestral veneration. The structure itself could be a microcosm of the cosmos, partitioning inside from outside – safety from the wilderness (Sampson, 1985).

3. Fish (Nun)

    - **Material Role**: Fish supplied vital protein, especially for communities near coasts or rivers. A consistent food source, fish supported maritime trade in Phoenicia and adjacent regions.

    - **Mythic Connotation**: Fish imagery appears in various creation tales, denoting primal waters or linking to goddesses of fertility and abundance. The fish's natural ability to thrive in the mysterious aquatic domain often carried symbolic weight (Daniels & Bright, 1996).

4. Door (Daleth)

- **Material Role**: Doors mark entry and exit, controlling access to dwellings, granaries, and communal halls.

- **Mythic Connotation**: The threshold is frequently a liminal space in the spiritual mindset of agrarian cultures – an interstice where one shifts between realms, be they mundane and sacred, interior and exterior, or known and unknown (Haarmann, 1990).

By assigning a pictographic or semi-pictographic glyph to each of these objects and employing them in writing, early scribes not only captured the lexical structure of their languages but also projected the fundamental **fabric of their world**. Each letter was a token of daily experience, bridging human concerns – food, shelter, livestock – with broader symbolic or divine significance.

Material-Spiritual Synergy

The synergy between **material** and **spiritual** elements in these glyphs is evident in how each object, while indispensable for survival, also drew upon a cosmic or ritual dimension:

1. Strength and "Ox"

- **Practical Necessity**: Oxen were the "muscle" behind plowing, effectively shaping the region's agricultural yield (Cross, 1980).

- **Spiritual Overtone**: In Near Eastern mythologies, bulls or oxen often represented virility or the thunderous strength of a storm deity. This dual role underscores how an everyday resource could symbolize cosmic potency (Haarmann, 1990).

2. Transition and "Door"

- **Practical Necessity**: Doors, shutters, and gates kept out predators and regulated communal life inside walled compounds.
- **Spiritual Overtone**: The "door" can metaphorically denote passage into new life phases – birth, death, or initiation. In some Levantine religious rites, passing through a threshold had ritual significance, marking transitions from profane to sacred space (Sass, 1988).

3. Sustenance and "Fish"

- **Practical Necessity**: Fish was a staple food, especially for coastal settlements. Fishing also became an economic linchpin through trade routes.
- **Spiritual Overtone**: In many ancient cultures, fish symbolize abundance, transformation (due to their life cycle), or the mysteries of the "deep." The watery domain was associated with creation narratives – e.g., chaotic waters preceding cosmic order, as in Mesopotamian and Canaanite myths (DeFrancis, 1989).

4. Refuge and "House"

- **Practical Necessity**: Houses provided safety from bandits, wild animals, and the elements. They consolidated kinship groups and social units.
- **Spiritual Overtone**: In numerous traditions, the house stands as a "sacred center," with a

hearth or shrine. The term "bayit" (related to Beth) even appears in some Semitic theological contexts, like "Beth-El," meaning "House of God" (Cross, 1980).

Each letter's name and iconographic form thus partook in a lived synergy: an **object** essential for daily life but resonant with deeper mythic or ritual frameworks. When scribes wrote these letters, they not only indicated speech sounds but invoked a shared cultural memory of how crucial these items were – both physically and spiritually (Sampson, 1985).

The Bronze Age Levant as Cultural Cradle

Historically, the **Bronze Age Levant** was a mosaic of city-states, tribal confederations, and trade outposts. Influences from neighboring Egypt, Mesopotamia, and the Aegean world converged in the Levantine corridor. In such a cosmopolitan environment, ideas about **agriculture, architecture, and religion** constantly circulated, intensifying the symbolic resonance of everyday realities. The script that would become Phoenician thus coalesced under conditions that demanded:

1. **Linguistic Efficiency**: A simplified sign system (the abjad) to record transactions, treaties, or dedications without mastering the more complex hieroglyphic or cuneiform scripts from neighboring powers (Daniels & Bright, 1996).

2. **Regional Identity**: A shared set of references unifying Levantine communities who recognized the same bedrock items – oxen, goats, houses, fences, water – even if they had minor dialectical differences.

3. **Ritual Practice**: Temple economies, sacrificial rites, and local gods anchored daily life in spiritual prac-

tice; thus, writing (including letter names) often doubled as a "sacred tool," capturing the tangible icons of worship (Cross, 1980).

The synergy manifested in the letter repertoire, mapping language to a microcosm of agrarian, pastoral, and spiritual lifeways. Each grapheme anchored the notion that literacy was not a purely **technical** skill but a domain bridging survival and the **transcendent** (Haarmann, 1990).

Emergence of Mythic Narratives

Even if the Phoenician script does not preserve extensive mythological texts the way Mesopotamian cuneiform or Egyptian hieroglyphs do, the implicit references in letter names point to **mythic resonance**. Scholars highlight how certain objects – like the **fence (Heth)** or the **camel (Gimel)** – appear repeatedly in Levantine legends surrounding migrations, covenant rituals, or heroic journeys (Sass, 1988). The fence might be seen as the boundary between civilization and wilderness, while the camel might symbolize the bridging of arid frontiers, an animal that laces together trade, culture, and cosmic significance:

- **Camel as "Gimel"**: Some interpret the root as connecting to generosity or recompense in Hebrew (the verb *gamal* can mean "to bestow," akin to a camel bearing goods). Mythically, it might also denote the bridging of distances – a motif in desert-based religious or heroic narratives (Cross, 1980).

- **Fence as "Heth"**: The dividing line between "inside" and "outside" resonates with mythic interpretations of order vs. chaos – settled farmland vs. the unknown. In certain rites, crossing a fence could be a symbolic act of venturing into the domain of the sacred or the demonic (Haarmann, 1990).

A Case for Ontolophemes

While direct textual evidence linking letters to formal myth is sparse, the **semantic fields** these items occupied in daily life overlapped with cosmic or ritual conceptions. The letter repertoire thus offered a compressed matrix – both a utilitarian script and a spiritual worldview in microcosm (Sampson, 1985).

Continuity and Transformation in Later Alphabets

When these Levantine scripts metamorphosed into Greek, Etruscan, Latin, and ultimately English alphabets, the **cultural reflection** dimension receded. Greek scribes repurposed some letters for vowels, overshadowing the earlier object references (DeFrancis, 1989). Latin expansions split single letters into multiples, focusing on phonetic coverage rather than referencing Bronze Age lifeways (Crystal, 2003). Despite this transformation, **traces** of the old synergy remain embedded in letter names like Alpha (ox) or Beta (house), even though few Greek or Latin speakers recognized their pastoral or mythic roots (Haarmann, 1990).

1. **Ox → Alpha**: As discussed, the letter name "Alpha" diverged from the Semitic understanding of an ox, reimagined for a purely phonetic vowel system. However, in certain esoteric traditions (including later Hermetic or Gnostic texts), letters like Alpha and Omega gained renewed cosmic significance, ironically echoing an older sense of "primal beginning" (Sass, 1988).

2. **House → Beta**: Greek usage divorced "house" from **Beta**; it was a sign for /b/. Yet in cultural memory, the letter name survived, bridging Greek orthography to Phoenician heritage.

3. **Fish → Nu, N**: Over centuries, "N" simply signified the nasal consonant, losing immediate ties to fish or

sustenance. Yet in early Christian symbolism, the fish (ichthys) re-emerged as a sacred sign, a curious parallel to the letter's ancient aquatic significance (Cross, 1980).

Modern Perspectives on Pastoral-Material Integration

From a modern vantage point, one might ask how relevant these Bronze Age references are in an era where alphabets are taught as neutral phonetic codes (Crystal, 2003). This question connects to the broader theme of **re-enchantment**: acknowledging that behind routine letters lurks a lattice of survival and spirituality that once guided entire cultures (Haarmann, 1990). Contemporary linguistic or conlang projects that aim to re-imbue letters with conceptual meaning effectively recapitulate this older synergy – crafting alphabets where each sign references objects, cultural stories, or metaphysical ideas (Peterson, 2015).

In historical scholarship, these references serve as **tools** for understanding how scripts originated not in the neat categories of modern linguistics but in the **material-spiritual** realities of early societies. Each letter is a relic of a world where an **ox** was not just a farm animal but a symbol of cosmic fertility, where a **door** was more than a plank of wood but a threshold to the unknown, and where **fish** could evoke the primal waters of creation (Daniels & Bright, 1996).

Concluding Thoughts

The **cultural reflection** embedded in the 21 ontic units provides a window into how **material life** and **spiritual imagination** intersected in early alphabetic traditions. Rather than perceiving alphabets as purely phonetic contrivances, we discern how each letter once anchored a vital piece of Bronze Age Levantine ecology: livestock, sustenance, architecture, trade routes, or bodily function. Simultaneously, these items carried mythic potential, hinting at cosmic energies or sacred thresholds (Sass, 1988).

In the journey from **Proto-Sinaitic** to **Phoenician** to **Greek** and **Latin**, the older synergy often faded from immediate awareness, supplanted by expansions and phonetic recalibrations. Yet the genealogical record remains: behind the familiar letters "A," "B," "C," "D," "M," "N," etc., lies an esoteric lattice of strength (ox), refuge (house), boundary (door), or water (mem). Recognizing this lattice enriches our contemporary engagement with the alphabet, transforming the mundane act of writing or reading into a subtle communion with millennia-old cultural memory (Crystal, 2003). Through this lens, the English script is not just 26 squiggles on a page but a living legacy of pastoral forging, symbolic transitions, and spiritual reflection – a synergy that once intimately bonded human hands, livestock, dwellings, and deities, interlacing language into the very texture of existence.

2. Role in Ritual and Magic

Beyond their function as markers of phonemes or mundane communicative tools, alphabets in many historical contexts have been viewed – and actively employed – as **incantatory** or **sacred** instruments for shaping reality. Across diverse cultures, letters were believed to channel cosmic forces, bridging mortal and divine spheres. This dimension of script is perhaps most evident in certain **runic** traditions, Hebrew **Kabbalah**, and a myriad of lesser-documented esoteric practices that treat the act of writing as a performative conjuration. In exploring this theme, we uncover parallels to the **Erilaz**, or "Runemaster," who stands as a potent example of the scribe-magician wielding letters with near-mythic potency (Dickins, 2002). This section delves into the ways letters transcend ordinary writing, embodying a form of ritual or magical technology that simultaneously encodes cosmic knowledge and invites the scribe to harness it.

Letters as Incantatory or Sacred Tools
2.1 The Notion of Script as Power

In many ancient cultures – Semitic, Germanic, Celtic, or otherwise – writing was rarely viewed as a neutral reflection of speech. Instead, it often **embodied** a tangible power, capable of **shaping events** or **summoning cosmic forces** (Sagdeev, 1989). This perspective thrived for several reasons:

1. **Scarcity of Literacy**: In preliterate or semiliterate communities, only a small elite possessed script knowledge. Mastery of writing appeared magical simply because it lay beyond the reach of most (Clunies Ross, 1998).

2. **Pictorial Origins**: Scripts that derived from iconic or symbolic imagery – like Egyptian hieroglyphs, early runes, or proto-Sinaitic glyphs – carried echoes of

their primal links to divine or natural forces. A letter might not merely mark a sound; it could stand for a protective or generative principle.

3. **Ritual Context**: Scribes frequently operated in or near temples, courts, or cultic centers. Their writing tasks often included making inscriptions for blessings, curses, or dedicatory formulae – further embedding script in a sacred or performative domain (Haarmann, 1990).

From this vantage, penning an inscription was akin to interlacing an incantation. Each **grapheme** served as a microcosm of larger cosmic forces, an **ontolopheme** referencing physical or spiritual realities. Whether the scribe's aim was to bless a king, consecrate a boundary, or curse an enemy, the letters themselves functioned as conduits for the scribe's will (Dickins, 2002).

2.2 Runic Practice

Among the most famous expressions of script-based magic in Europe is **runic** practice. The term "rune" traces back to Proto-Germanic *rūnō*, meaning "secret" or "mystery," highlighting the esoteric aura surrounding these letters (Page, 1999). By the early centuries CE, Germanic tribes had developed the **Elder Futhark** – a script of around 24 runes, each associated with a name, a phonetic value, and often a symbolic domain. Epigraphic finds show that runes were carved on **amulets**, **weapons**, **tombstones**, and **wooden talismans**, presumably to channel protective or destructive energies.

1. **Incantatory Inscriptions**: Sagas and legal codes from early medieval Scandinavia hint at runic spells for healing, warding off evil, or binding an enemy (Clunies Ross, 1998). For instance, amulets with runic formulas often prayed for divine or supernatural

assistance, merging the scribe's craft with the sphere of ritual invocation.

2. **Runes as Gateways**: Many runologists argue that each rune was far more than a sign for a speech sound; it was a container for potent cosmic truths. **Fehu** (ᚠ) could denote cattle and wealth, but also prosperity, luck, and fertility. **Ansuz** (ᚨ), referencing the god Odin or "divine breath," invoked mental insight or communication from higher realms (Page, 1999).

Hence, runic writing illustrates that, in certain societies, **letters functioned as magical glyphs** capable of shaping fate. Though the exact details of runic magic are debated – owing to partial textual evidence – what remains is a robust tradition attributing letters with incantatory might. This synergy between reading, carving, and chanting underscores the deep hold alphabets can exert on spiritual imagination (Sagdeev, 1989).

2.3 Hebrew Kabbalah and Letter Mysticism

Another landmark tradition associating letters with divine or mystical power is **Hebrew Kabbalah**, especially as articulated in texts like the **Sefer Yetzirah** (often dated between the 3rd and 6th centuries CE) and later in medieval Kabbalistic writings (Scholem, 1969). These works view the **22 letters** of the Hebrew alphabet as building blocks of creation – conduits through which the divine presence shaped the cosmos. Their resonance parallels the earlier notion of ontolophemes, albeit in a more openly theological framework.

1. **Letters as Creative Agents**: The Sefer Yetzirah posits that God employed Hebrew letters to **speak** the world into being. Each letter, from **Aleph** (א) to **Tav**

(ת), corresponds to cosmic powers – whether elemental, planetary, or zodiacal (Kaplan, 1997).

2. **Permutations and Combinations**: Kabbalists delve into permutations of letters to uncover hidden layers of meaning in sacred texts – often believing that rearranging letter sequences can **reveal** or **unlock** spiritual truths.

3. **Letter-Based Rituals**: Medieval and early modern Kabbalists sometimes prescribed letter-based meditations or invocations, where the scribe's attention to each stroke, shape, and name of the letter invoked particular angelic or divine forces (Scholem, 1969).

Hebrew letter mysticism underscores a direct continuity with the worldview that sees alphabets not as arbitrary codes, but as **crystallized forms** of creation's blueprint. The scribe or mystic becomes a caretaker of that blueprint, able to manipulate it for revelation, healing, or communion with the divine.

The Erilaz (Runemaster) Parallel: The Scribe as Magician

Across these cultural landscapes, from runic carvings to Kabbalistic incantations, a figure emerges who **possesses** and **exploits** the deeper properties of letters: the **Erilaz** in Germanic tradition, paralleled by scribes, priests, or magicians in other societies (Dickins, 2002).

3.1 Defining the Erilaz

In early runic inscriptions, the term *erilaz* appears, frequently interpreted as "runemaster," "rune-cutter," or "one who knows runes." Such individuals presumably occupied a liminal role – part craftsman, part seer. The title connotes mastery of esoteric knowledge, bridging the mundane task of carving letters with the spiritual act of conjuring or controlling forces (Clunies Ross, 1998). This resonates strongly with the biblical or apocryphal image of scribes in the Near East, many of whom were religious functionaries as well as bureaucratic accountants (Sagdeev, 1989).

1. **Literacy as Arcane Power**: In a largely oral society, any ability to write – particularly in mysterious runic letters – conferred an aura of the supernatural. The Erilaz might be approached to craft protective staves, interpret omens, or embed curses in carved formulas.

2. **Resonance with Kabbalistic Scribes**: Like the Kabbalist meticulously drawing each Hebrew letter in adherence to halakhic and mystical stipulations, the Erilaz approached each rune as an instrument of cosmic interplay. The shapes, angles, and even the direction of carving all carried weight (Scholem, 1969).

3.2 Scribes as Magicians in Broader Contexts

Although the term "Erilaz" is specific to Germanic tradition, **scribe-magicians** appear in many literate cultures:

- **Egyptian Hierogrammateis**: Temple scribes who carved hieroglyphs believed each glyph retained a fragment of divine potency, bridging mortal realms with the pantheon (Manley, 2012).

- **Mesopotamian Ašipu** or incantation priests: Cuneiform spells, etched onto clay tablets, invoked gods and spirits to dispel ailments or curses, underscoring how writing and magical practice often merged (Bottéro, 2001).

- **Chinese Fangshi** or ritual specialists: In some Daoist traditions, specialized glyphs or "talismans" (fu) combined a script-like form with calligraphic invocation, effectively turning written signs into magical seals (Kohn, 2000).

A Case for Ontolophemes

In each instance, the scribe's authority stemmed from the capacity to connect a letter's **shape**, **name**, and **conceptual** dimension with an intangible but potent domain. The Erilaz stands as a Northern European archetype, while the Kabbalist scribe exemplifies the Judaic variant; yet across the board, the principle remains: through writing, the scribe channels universal energies.

Letters as Incantatory Keys: Cultural Universality

When we compare runic incantations, Hebrew letter mysticism, and parallel phenomena in Egyptian or Chinese contexts, a **cultural universality** emerges: alphabets or writing systems can function as **keys** to ritual empowerment (Clunies Ross, 1998). Whether we label them "ontolophemes" or "graphemes," their usage in **spells** or **sacred inscriptions** underscores a few core truths:

1. **Script as Threshold**: Writing stands at the boundary between **matter** (the inscribed surface) and **spirit** (the invoked or evoked power).

2. **Mastery Requires Initiation**: One rarely learns runic magic or Kabbalistic letter manipulation solely through rote literacy; deeper teaching or spiritual apprenticeship is implied. This fosters a sense of "secrets of letters" preserved for the initiated (Kaplan, 1997; Page, 1999).

3. **Performative Efficacy**: The act of writing, carving, or chanting the letters is itself believed to **perform** an effect – warding off evil, attracting blessings, revealing hidden knowledge. The letter's shape or sound resonates with the cosmos, prompting a real transformation in the physical or spiritual plane.

By capturing these universal lines, we see that writing transcends its **mundane** function. When harnessed in ritual or magic, letters become **living incantations** – and the scribe becomes a caretaker of a cosmic alphabet, interlacing intangible energies into the tangible world (Dickins, 2002).

Concluding Reflections

The **role of letters in ritual and magic** thus provides a sharp departure from the modern, largely exoteric teaching of alphabets as neutral phonetic codes. Throughout history, and across multiple civilizations, letters have been revered as **active agents** in shaping or negotiating cosmic and terrestrial realities (Sagdeev, 1989). The runes exemplify this in Northern Europe, merging symbol and incantation in the figure of the Erilaz – a runemaster wielding near-sorcerous power through carved staves. Hebrew Kabbalah, meanwhile, refracts a parallel vision in which each grapheme is a microcosm of the divine creative process. Similar patterns arise wherever writing melds with spiritual practice, from Egyptian temple carvings to Chinese Daoist talismans.

Not merely a historical curiosity, this perspective enriches our present understanding of alphabets as **ontological** or **mythic** frameworks, bridging everyday literacy and sacred quest. In the runic worldview, carving a letter was tantamount to conjuring the essence it symbolized – an attitude echoed in the Kabbalist's fervor that each Hebrew letter enshrines the forces that shaped the universe. Together, these traditions confirm that writing can function as both **communication** and **incantation**, and the scribe – like the Erilaz – remains the liminal figure bridging sound, shape, and cosmic design (Haarmann, 1990). Whether we glimpse these beliefs in archaic inscriptions or medieval grimoires, the magical dimension of writing affirms the potent synergy between **letter** and **reality**: an ancient synergy that continues to fascinate scholars, esoteric practitioners, and curious minds alike.

Icosikaihexagon and Icosihenagon

V. THE 26 VISIBLE LETTERS (ICOSIKAIHEXAGON)

A Case for Ontolophemes

A. Practical Exoteric Dimension

The **English alphabet**, consisting of 26 letters from **A** to **Z**, appears deceptively simple – a fixed lineup on classroom charts, a standard sequence in children's songs, and the bedrock of written communication for hundreds of millions of people worldwide. Yet, as previously explored, this 26-letter set (the **icosikaihexagon**) is the final, exoteric form of a system whose **ancestral substratum** is far smaller and more conceptually anchored in ancient agrarian life. In this section, we focus on the **practical exoteric dimension** of these letters, examining how they function in modern English orthography, and then contrast their visible usage with the deeper, hidden genealogies we have traced (Crystal, 2003). The tension between **simulacrum** (the surface array of 26 graphemes) and **archetype** (the smaller proto-ontology behind them) underscores the dual reality of the alphabet: an everyday tool that nonetheless carries echoes of an ancient cosmic map.

1. English Orthography

1.1 Each Letter's Common IPA Values

At the broadest level, when English speakers learn to read and write, they encounter 26 distinct letters assigned to a variable set of **phonemes** – that is, the smallest contrastive sounds in English. While the alphabetic principle suggests that each letter should map neatly to a particular sound, centuries of historical shifts, loanwords, and dialectical variations have led to a more **complex** reality (Crystal, 2003). Below, we offer an overview of each letter's most frequent **IPA** (International Phonetic Alphabet) values in contemporary mainstream English, though with the caveat that actual pronunciations can vary widely across dialects (Wells, 1982).

Icosikaihexagon and Icosihenagon

1. A

- Commonly /æ/ (as in *cat*), /eɪ/ (as in *name*), /ɑː/ (as in *father* in many dialects), /ɔː/ (in *water* in some accents), or even /ə/ (in unstressed syllables, e.g., *about*).
- This multiplicity arises from historical sound shifts (the Great Vowel Shift, among others) and borrowings from French, Latin, or Greek.

2. B

- Typically /b/ (as in *bat*, *baby*).
- English rarely uses "B" for other sounds, though it may be silent in certain words (e.g., *doubt*, *lamb*) due to historical developments (Carney, 1994).

3. C

- Often /k/ (as in *cat*) or /s/ (as in *city*). In a small set of words, it can appear in digraphs (e.g., *ch* as in /tʃ/, *machine*, *chord*) or even /ʃ/ in some loanwords (*cello*).
- Reflects the etymological complexity of English, as words from Latin, Greek, Old Norse, and French shaped orthographic norms (Crystal, 2003).

4. D

- Usually /d/ (as in *dog*), with minor variations in voiced alveolar stops, and occasional silent usage (e.g., *Wednesday* in some dialects).

5. E

- Commonly /ɛ/ (as in *bed*), /iː/ (in "e"-final words like *mere* historically, though merging can occur), /eɪ/ in some loanwords (like *café*).
- Also ubiquitous as the final "silent E," which modifies vowel length in preceding syllables (e.g., *rat* vs. *rate*).

6. F
    - Typically /f/ (as in *fan*, *off*). Rarely other values (save for older ephemeral usage in Middle English or dialectal phenomena).

7. G
    - Often /g/ (as in *go*, *bag*), /dʒ/ in certain words of French origin (e.g., *genre*), or silent in words like *gnome*, reflecting historical transformations.

8. H
    - /h/ (as in *hat*), but silent in many contexts (*honest*, *hour*, *ghost*).
    - Varied presence in digraphs: *ch* (/tʃ/), *th* (/θ/ or /ð/), *gh* (historically /x/, often silent or /f/ in some archaic forms).

9. I
    - Can be /ɪ/ (as in *bit*), /aɪ/ (as in *site*), /iː/ (as in *machine*), or /ɪ/ in unstressed endings (*happiness*).
    - Significant variation tied to the Great Vowel Shift and French/Latin loanwords.

10. J

- Principally /dʒ/ (as in *judge*, *jam*), though some loanwords adopt /ʒ/ or other minority variants (e.g., *Jacques* in a French context).

11. K

- /k/ (as in *kite*, *back*). Frequently silent (e.g., *knight*, *knife*), a vestige of Old English orthography where *k* was once pronounced (Scragg, 1974).

12. L

- /l/ (as in *love*, *all*). Can appear as a "dark L" (velarized) in coda positions (e.g., *milk*, *full*). Possibly silent in words like *could*, *would*, *should*.

13. M

- /m/ (as in *man*, *seem*). Rarely deviates; one of the more consistent grapheme-phoneme pairings.

14. N

- /n/ (as in *not*, *can*). With certain morphological patterns, it merges or assimilates with following consonants (e.g., in *thank*, historically /n/ + /k/).

15. O

- Highly variable: /ɒ/ (in British *hot*), /oʊ/ (in American *hope*), /ɔː/ (in *thought*, *law*), or /ə/ in unstressed positions (e.g., *today*).

- Reflects extensive lexical borrowing and dialectical evolution (Wells, 1982).

16. P

- /p/ (as in *pin*, *cup*). Again, fairly consistent, though silent in some Greek-based words like *pneumonia*.

17. Q

A Case for Ontolophemes

- Almost always appears in the digraph **qu**, representing /kw/ (as in *queen*, *quick*). In borrowed words, it may reduce to /k/ (*conquer*, *bouquet*).

18. R

- /ɹ/ (in most American and many modern English dialects). Non-rhotic accents (e.g., RP British) restrict *R* to onset or certain linking positions.

- Historically, /r/ varied from alveolar taps or trills in older or dialectal forms (Crystal, 2003).

19. S

- Typically /s/ (as in *sit*, *hiss*), /z/ (in *dogs*, *was*), or /ʃ/ (in *sugar*, *sure*). Appears in digraphs *sh* (/ʃ/), *sc* (/s/ or /ʃ/), etc.

20. T

- Usually /t/ (as in *top*, *cat*). Undergoes softening in certain contexts (e.g., /tʃ/ in words like *nature* for some dialects, or flapped in American English after vowels: *latter* → /ˈlæɾɚ/).

21. U

- /uː/ (as in *flute*), /ʊ/ (in *put*, depending on dialect), /juː/ (as in *use*), or /ʌ/ (in *cut*, spelled <u> in many words).

- Complexity arises from Middle English mergers, Great Vowel Shift changes, and morphological expansions (Carney, 1994).

22. V

- /v/ (as in *van*, *love*). Historically absent in earlier Old English alphabets, introduced from French and Latin usage.

23. W

- /w/ (as in *win*, *cow*), reflecting its Germanic heritage as "double-u." Sometimes silent in *wrap*, *write*, or altered in some dialect forms.

24. X

- Commonly /ks/ (as in *box*, *fox*), /gz/ (as in *exact*), or occasionally /z/ (as in *xylophone*).
- A letter with broad assimilation patterns in Greek and Latin loanwords (Crystal, 2003).

25. Y

- /j/ (as in *yes*), /ɪ/ or /i/ in final unstressed syllables (*happy* → /ˈhæpi/), or /aɪ/ (in *myth* for some speakers).
- Historically linked to Greek upsilon, used for loanwords in Latin, and thus integrated into English for various phonetic roles.

26. Z

- /z/ (as in *zoo*, *buzz*), or /ts/ /dz/ in a few borrowed words from foreign tongues (*pizza*, though English typically reanalyzes it as /ˈpiːtsə/). Rare in Old English, reintroduced post-Norman era.

Although we list these major correspondences, the actual mapping from letter to sound in English is notoriously **irregular** compared to languages like Spanish or Finnish, which maintain more consistent grapheme-phoneme correspondences (Carney, 1994). Over centuries, English orthography has become a **mosaic** of historical residues, morphological constraints, foreign orthographic traditions, and dialectical variation (Crystal, 2003).

1.2 Spelling as a Highly Variable Mapping from Grapheme to Sound

The complexity of English spelling has long been a subject of **reform attempts** and comedic laments: George Bernard Shaw famously highlighted how the word *fish* might theoretically be spelled "ghoti" if one aggregated English's silent or unusual grapheme uses (scraping /f/ from *enough*, /ɪ/ from *women*, and /ʃ/ from *nation*) (Sampson, 1985). While humorous, such examples underscore a central fact about **exoteric** English orthography: it represents a **superimposed** scheme that only loosely corresponds to modern phonetics (Crystal, 2003).

1. **Historical Layers**: From Old English (Anglo-Saxon runes and Roman letters) to Middle English (Norman French influences) to Early Modern English (Renaissance Latin borrowings), each era left behind orthographic footprints.

2. **Morphophonemic Considerations**: Some spellings preserve morphological relationships across word families – e.g., *electric* and *electricity* – despite evolving pronunciation, resulting in mismatch between grapheme and sound (Carney, 1994).

3. **Dialects and Standardization**: The printing press, introduced by William Caxton around 1476, standardized a single dialect (East Midlands/London). Pronunciation, however, continued to evolve, locking archaic spellings in place (Crystal, 2003).

Hence, the average English user wields a 26-letter system without cognizance that many letters serve multiple phonetic roles, reflect older morphological states, or echo foreign orthographic patterns. At a purely functional level, the exoteric dimension suffices to communicate meaning – readers become adept at memorizing irregular spellings, and context usually clarifies homographs or ambiguous letters.

Yet the phenomenon of orthographic "chaos" hints at deeper layers of **historical** and **conceptual** complexity.

2. Simulacrum vs. Archetype

2.1 Our Daily Usage of Letters Hides Deeper Connections

Given the exoteric perspective, an everyday English speaker sees **26 distinct letters** forming a **closed set**: the impetus is purely functional – "A" stands for certain vowels, "B" stands for /b/, "C" stands for /k/ or /s/ and so forth. Rarely does one pause to wonder why "W" is spelled as a "double-u," or why "G" and "C" are intimately linked in alphabetical ancestry. For practical literacy, these questions appear irrelevant. The teacher's main priority is ensuring that students can read and write effectively, navigating the known irregularities of English (Crystal, 2003).

However, from an **etymological** and **historical** vantage, many letters are not truly distinct origins but **branches** from fewer conceptual lineages. As elaborated in earlier sections, "U," "V," "W," and "Y" all trace to the same Phoenician glyph, *Waw*. "I" and "J" share an origin in *Yod*. "C" and "G" converge in the archaic shape for *Gimel*. By the time these shapes funneled through Greek, Etruscan, and Latin, they splintered into multiple forms, each reinterpreted for new phonemic contexts (Daniels & Bright, 1996). The modern user seldom perceives this genealogical unity. **"A"** is just "A," unconnected (in the user's mind) to an ancient "ox" concept (*Aleph*), while "W" might appear an entirely separate letter, unmoored from its "hook/peg" Semitic root (*Waw*).

In effect, the **icosikaihexagon** – 26 outward edges – functions as a **simulacrum**: a visually expanded system that conceals deeper genealogical lines merging at 21 or so "ontic seeds." The **archetype** of the alphabet, the hidden ontology we have traced from proto-Sinaitic and Phoenician, remains invisible to most contemporary eyes (Cross, 1980). We might

A Case for Ontolophemes

type thousands of words a day without suspecting we repeatedly evoke archaic references to livestock, shelter, or fundamental cosmic categories.

2.2 Yet the Shapes and Letters Remain Carriers of Ancestral Memory

Despite the modern user's lack of awareness, these shapes and letters persist as **carriers** of ancestral memory. They are **palimpsests**, each layered with centuries of morphological transformations. A letter like **A** still vaguely recalls the shape of an ox head in some stylized fonts, though heavily abstracted. The crossbar might evoke horns, the angled lines a stylized skull. Meanwhile, letters like **B** can hint at the segmented "house plan," though it is drastically changed by Roman stylization and subsequent printing standardizations (Sass, 1988).

1. **Typographic Evolution**: The transition from scribal manuscripts to movable type, from Gothic blackletter to Times New Roman, further abstracted letter forms, rendering them more standardized, less iconic (Carney, 1994).

2. **Echoes in Letter Names**: Greek retains "Alpha," "Beta," "Gamma," "Delta," faintly echoing ox, house, camel, door. English letter names like "A," "B," "C," "D" are shortened adaptations from the same chain, though we rarely recall the older references (Crystal, 2003).

3. **Esoteric or Scholarly Rediscovery**: From the 19th century onward, philologists, archaeologists, and epigraphers have reconnected these letters to their original pictographic or conceptual forms. This knowledge remains specialized, typically absent in basic literacy instruction, but it reaffirms that the

shapes we take for granted are historically **charged** with significance (Cross, 1980).

The gap between exoteric usage and esoteric ancestry forms a kind of **cultural amnesia**: we employ letters daily, thinking of them as neutral signs, yet they represent a living genealogical chain stretching back to pastoral societies whose worldview hinged on "oxen, houses, fish, water, doors, and the rest" (Daniels & Bright, 1996). The alphabet thus stands at a crossroads, where pragmatic modern reading/writing collides with the half-forgotten vestiges of Bronze Age symbolism.

The Simulacrum–Archetype Tension: A Closer Look

To elaborate further on how the modern 26 letters embody a **simulacrum** as opposed to the older archetype, one might consider:

1. **Numerical Mismatch**: Phoenician had 22 letters, each referencing a discrete concept (ox, house, camel, door, fish, etc.). Through expansions, English ended up with 26 letters, but not four new conceptual seeds. Instead, single Phoenician glyphs gave rise to multiple Roman letters: "I" → "I/J," "V" → "U/V/W/Y." The result is a mismatch: more letters, same conceptual basis.

2. **Phonological Overload**: The exoteric English system lumps multiple phonemes under one letter or merges different letters to represent the same sound (e.g., "C" can be /k/ or /s/). This conflation arises from orthographic accidents and historical layering, not from new conceptual expansions.

3. **Obscured Ontology**: The simulacrum fosters the illusion that English has 26 "fundamentally distinct" letters. In reality, from the vantage of ancestral mean-

ing, many of these are duplicates or siblings – like multiple branches from one trunk (Cross, 1980).

Example: "W" as a Case Study

Take **W**: to an English speaker, it is the **23rd** letter, used to represent the approximant /w/ in words like *win*, *twist*, *water*. It has no obvious link to **U** or **V** in daily usage. Teachers instruct children to see it as a single letter, albeit strangely spelled as "double-u." The average user seldom ponders its shape or name.

- **Genealogical Lens**: Delving deeper, "W" emerged from a **split** in medieval Latin usage. Since Latin had no /w/ phoneme, scribes writing Germanic tongues doubled the "V" shape to represent /w/. Over time, "UU" (uu) stylized into "w," retaining the name "double-u" (Crystal, 2003).

- **Phoenician Root**: Both "U" (the vowel) and "V" (the consonant) trace to the same Semitic letter, *Waw* (𐤅), meaning "hook/peg." The phoneme /v/ in classical Latin was a minor variant, eventually diverging from /u/ in medieval practice. From that single glyph grew not only "U" and "V," but also "W" and "Y."

- **Conclusion**: The modern exoteric vantage sees "W" as a distinct entity in the 26-letter pantheon. The hidden archetype reveals it as one more branch of *Waw*, conceptually referencing a "peg" – a mundane yet crucial item for tent-based or early Levantine societies. This synergy between ancient "peg" and modern /w/ underscores the simulacrum: more letters, no new conceptual origin.

Educational and Cultural Implications

One might wonder whether it matters that English orthography is a simulacrum concealing older archetypes. **Educationally**, many argue that acknowledging the deeper genealogies could foster a richer sense of literacy. Instead of viewing letters purely as inert shapes, students might appreciate the **historical journeys** these symbols took: how "A" was once an ox, how "B" a house, and so forth (Zakaluk & Samuels, 1988). Such an approach could demystify certain irregularities, demonstrating that "C" and "G" share a root, "I" and "J" share another, "U," "V," "W," "Y" yet another. The result might not fix English spelling but could sharpen learners' meta-linguistic awareness.

Culturally, reacquainting ourselves with the archetypal dimension can re-enchant daily reading and writing. The act of typing or handwriting might become more meaningful when we recall that "D" once signified a door or threshold, that "M" was water. This resonates with broader movements in the humanities that champion **historical consciousness** – the notion that deep genealogies enrich our connection to language, culture, and identity (Crystal, 2003; Sampson, 1985).

The Tension in Contemporary Linguistics

Contemporary linguistics often adopts a synchronic perspective, analyzing how speakers use letters **now**, with minimal reference to historical or symbolic backstories (Chomsky & Halle, 1968). Orthographers might propose incremental reforms to reduce grapheme-phoneme mismatch, but rarely do they address the archaic ontology behind the letters. Meanwhile, historical linguistics or philology uncovers these genealogies and conceptual seeds but seldom influences mainstream orthographic policy or literacy education (Daniels & Bright, 1996). Thus, the tension remains:

A Case for Ontolophemes

1. **Pragmatic Uniformity**: In daily life, English orthography is standardized around the 26-letter set, taught as a finite inventory with certain "quirks."

2. **Genealogical Complexity**: Behind that uniform set stands an older mosaic of duplications and expansions, all anchored in an original 21–22 letter system naming everyday objects of Bronze Age Levantine life.

From a purely communicative standpoint, modern usage works. The exoteric system is adequate to represent most English words (with some guesswork about vowels and irregular forms). From a genealogical vantage, though, the 26 letters are far from truly distinct: they are a **simulacrum** shaped by centuries of historical happenstance, overshadowing the simpler cosmic or agrarian blueprint that once unified them (Cross, 1980).

Why the Simulacrum–Archetype Duality Matters

The distinction between **simulacrum** and **archetype** is not merely academic. It casts light on how we **conceptualize** writing itself:

1. **Loss of Sacred or Symbolic Resonance**: In many ancient and medieval contexts, letters carried near-magical weight. By the time of modern secular education, alphabets are taught as neutral technology, stripped of cosmic references – yet these references remain "under the hood" if we look closely (DeFrancis, 1989).

2. **Potential for Interdisciplinary Inquiry**: Scholars in anthropology, semiotics, and cultural studies can glean insights into how societies transform sacred symbols into everyday tools. The 26 English letters

exemplify the final stage of transformation, where the user no longer recognizes the symbolic origins.

3. **Creative Reclamation**: Conlangers, esoteric practitioners, or educators might reclaim these archaic references to reanimate letters with new or old symbolic weight, bridging ancient ontology and contemporary expression (Peterson, 2015). This bridging can reawaken a sense of wonder in tasks as mundane as writing an email.

Hence, acknowledging the deeper genealogical or esoteric dimension of the 26 letters can refresh our perspective on literacy, bridging the everyday exoteric function with a newly appreciated historical depth. It demonstrates that even the simplest act of writing "A, B, C…" partakes in a tradition stretching back millennia, one that once enumerated the "ox, house, camel, door, fish" that structured a Bronze Age cosmos (Sass, 1988).

Broader Connections: Technology, Orthography, and the Future

In the digital age, we constantly **type** these 26 letters, a process made frictionless by QWERTY keyboards, autocorrect algorithms, and a global English lingua franca. Technological developments accelerate orthographic standardization and obscure historical complexities, as software and social media push for quick, uniform text. Meanwhile, the hidden genealogical lines remain known primarily to specialists – philologists, epigraphers, or conlang hobbyists (Daniels & Bright, 1996).

Could the tension between simulacrum and archetype change in the future? Possibly. A renewed fascination with **etymological apps**, **virtual museums**, or **AR experiences** might bring these genealogies to the forefront, letting everyday users see how "A" morphs from an ox head, or "U, V, W,

Y" share a single Phoenician root (Cross, 1980). Interactive technologies could unite exoteric usage with the archetypal lattice that once shaped these graphemes, forging a literacy that is historically and cosmically aware.

Even so, absent a broad educational shift, most users will continue to see 26 distinct letters as a simple, pragmatic set. The simulacrum remains the **operational** truth: we do not question why "J" and "I" differ, or how "C" and "G" share an origin, so long as we can read and write effectively. Our "A" remains a letter for various vowels, not a symbol for an ox or cosmic fertility. The archetype stands behind the scenes, accessible but seldom invoked.

Conclusion

In summation, the **icosikaihexagon** of modern English orthography is the exoteric face of a more compact ancestral domain. Each of the 26 letters – A through Z – carries multiple IPA values, shaped by centuries of historical layering, loanword assimilation, and morphological considerations (Crystal, 2003). The result is a graphically stable but phonetically chaotic system that demands extensive memorization and contextual inference from users. Yet beneath this labyrinth of spelling irregularities and expansions lies a smaller, older **archetype**, reflecting the agrarian-pastoral worldview of Bronze Age Levantine societies (Cross, 1980).

This tension between **simulacrum** and **archetype** goes beyond orthographic curiosity. It unveils how alphabets can drift from their conceptual moorings over millennia, such that a single Phoenician glyph (e.g., *Waw*) can branch into four or more Roman letters, and an "ox" shape can become the letter "A" used for five or six different vowel sounds. For functional literacy in the 21st century, the exoteric 26 letters suffice, but as historical or esoteric inquiry shows, they remain impregnated with an archaic memory – a memory of houses, doors, fish, water, and cosmic forces.

Revisiting this memory fosters a richer engagement with literacy: no longer is writing a purely mechanical act but the modern tip of an **immense genealogical iceberg**, whose foundation was laid by scribes, traders, and agrarian peoples thousands of years ago (Daniels & Bright, 1996). By acknowledging the hidden lines that unify "I" and "J," or "U, V, W, Y," we see that the 26 visible sides of English orthography form a **closed polygon** superimposed on a simpler, older geometry. This geometry, the icosihenagon, enumerates fundamental objects and concepts, bridging the mundane (fences, camels, fish) with the cosmic or ritual domain.

Whether or not the average writer or student ever learns of these origins, the script itself testifies to a continuity between **past** and **present**. The shapes we use to email, text, or craft entire novels were once pictographs signifying the bedrock realities of desert herders and city dwellers on the eastern Mediterranean littoral. Thus, the "A, B, C..." that populate our screens and pages are the outward exoteric shell of an older, more unified set of cosmic or agrarian references. If we choose to see it, each letter stands as a subtle relic of a lost worldview – where an **ox** was not just a resource but also a symbol of generative might, and where the **house** was not merely a building but the microcosm of family and spiritual identity (Cross, 1980; Sass, 1988).

In the end, this duality – **26** exoteric letters overshadowing a genealogical 21 or 22 – does not hamper everyday communication, but it does remind us that writing is never "just writing." It is a palimpsest of human experience, bridging epochs, languages, and conceptual frames. By peeling back the exoteric simulacrum, we reconnect with the archetype, glimpsing how even the simplest act of writing one's name can trace a lineage back to **doors** and **water**, **oxen** and **fish**, **ritual** and **magic**. Recognizing that legacy can enrich

A Case for Ontolophemes

our sense of literacy, turning it from a routine skill into an ongoing dance with history, memory, and the enduring power of symbolic forms (Crystal, 2003; Daniels & Bright, 1996).

B. Case Studies

Even though the English alphabet presents itself as a coherent set of twenty-six letters in a single sequence, its internal genealogies diverge into multiple channels traceable to distinct or overlapping ancient roots. In certain cases, a single Phoenician glyph spawned multiple Roman letters; in others, Greek intermediaries repurposed or merged letter forms, obscuring the lines of descent. By exploring specific examples, we see how original concepts – like "spine," "peg," or "hand" – splintered into various orthographic outcomes in today's writing systems (Cross, 1980; Daniels & Bright, 1996). This section spotlights three illustrative case studies: the letter **X** (linked to Greek **Chi** or **Xi** and Phoenician **Samekh**), the group **U, V, W, Y** (descended from **Waw**), and the pair **I, J** (descending from **Yod**).

1. X (Chi / Xi / Samekh)

Possibly "spine" or "fish backbone;" now just /ks/.

1.1 Phoenician Origins and Ambiguities

The letter **X** in the Latin script has a complex lineage tied ultimately to Greek letters – particularly **Chi (X)** and **Xi (Ξ)** – but also has roots that many scholars trace back to Phoenician **Samekh (⟊)** (Sass, 1988). *Samekh* is often translated as "fish spine," "support," or "spine/backbone." In Semitic linguistics, the name likely derives from the root *s-m-k*, which connotes "to support" or "sustain." Early pictographic or stylized forms might have depicted a vertebral column or structural prop. Some older hypotheses suggest a fish skeleton as well, signifying the bony ridge of a fish's dorsal side (Cross, 1980). The precise image is debated, but the essential notion is that *Samekh* symbolized a **supportive, skeletal, or spined** object.

A Case for Ontolophemes

From a conceptual standpoint, the letter thus signaled the idea of a **structural backbone**. When Phoenician letters passed into the Greek repertoire, changes arose to match Greek phonology. Greek had multiple sibilants or affricates that needed representation, and **Xi (Ξ)** was used for the cluster /ks/, while **Chi (X)** eventually stood for an aspirated /kʰ/ (in classical Greek). The shape or name no longer explicitly conjured "spine" or "fish skeleton"; instead, it addressed phonetic demands in Greek (Sampson, 1985).

1.2 Greek Transfers to Latin

In early Greek usage, **Xi (Ξ)** was sometimes employed as the letter after Nu (N), capturing /ks/ in the alphabetic order (Daniels & Bright, 1996). By the time the alphabet passed through Etruscan intermediaries to Latin, the Romans faced various choices for how to represent /ks/ or /cs/ clusters. They adopted a letter shape akin to Greek Xi or Chi but integrated it into their standard 21–23 letter system as **X**, signifying /ks/. This allocation occurred fairly early in Latin, as words like *lux* (/lʊks/ "light") show. The letter's name in Latin likely derived from the Greek letter's name or a local adaptation thereof, but none of the older "backbone" connotation remained active in the Roman context (Cross, 1980).

1.3 Modern English Usage

Today, in English, **X** stands for /ks/ (as in *box*, /bɒks/ or /bɑːks/), occasionally /gz/ (as in *examine*, /ɪgˈzæmɪn/), or even /z/ in a few exotic loanwords (*xylophone*, /ˈzaɪləfoʊn/ in some dialects). This range of values highlights the patchwork nature of English spelling, with "X" deriving from multiple lexical streams (Crystal, 2003). Nowhere does the letter evoke "spine" or "support" to the modern user, relegating that older concept to the domain of specialized philological knowledge. Viewed genealogically, we can see that an ancient sense of structural backbone or fish skeleton collapsed into a purely phonetic placeholder for a /ks/ cluster in Latin script – a transformation that exemplifies how an **ontic** reference can vanish under layers of phonemic adaptation (Sass, 1988).

1.4 Symbolic Residues and Cultural Echoes

In esoteric or poetic reappropriations, some conlangers or mystics reinvest "X" with the sense of crossing, intersection, or support, reminiscent of the letter's archaic skeleton imagery (DeFrancis, 1989). Nonetheless, mainstream orthography retains no memory of the fish backbone or spine concept. **X** stands out as a case where the morphological shape (two intersecting strokes) indirectly recalls a crossing or structure, but the deeper genealogical meaning – *Samekh*, "spine" – resides behind centuries of orthographic evolution (Cross, 1980).

2. U, V, W, Y (All from Waw)

All from "hook/peg," yet have distinct modern roles.

2.1 Phoenician *Waw* (𐤅): A Simple Peg or Hook

Among the most striking examples of letter proliferation is the cluster **U, V, W, Y**, all rooted in the Phoenician glyph *Waw* (𐤅). In Semitic languages, *Waw* originally denoted the consonant /w/ or served as a "mater lectionis" for certain vowel contexts. The name *Waw* – meaning "hook," "peg," or "nail" – likely reflected an ancient pictograph showing a vertical stake or peg (Sass, 1988). This was a crucial object in pastoral societies, used to secure tents or equipment. Tents, as ephemeral but essential homes in desert or steppe environments, required pegs hammered into the ground. Thus, the letter symbolically pointed to the concept of fastening or stability (Cross, 1980).

2.2 Greek and Latin Transmissions

When Phoenician letters entered Greek, *Waw* did not always find a direct one-to-one match. Some dialects adopted it as **digamma** (ϝ), used for the /w/ sound in archaic Greek

A Case for Ontolophemes

(Mycenaean or certain dialects like Laconian). However, digamma gradually fell out of use in classical Ionian-Attic Greek, which lacked a strong /w/ phoneme. Meanwhile, in archaic Etruscan or early Latin, the letter that came to represent the /u/ or /v/ phoneme was adapted from a shape akin to digamma (Sampson, 1985).

By classical Latin times, the letter written as "V" served for both /u/ (vowel) and /v/ (consonant). This single letter "V" might appear in inscriptions like "AVGVSTVS" (Augustus), read as /augʊstʊs/ in classical pronunciation. The shape, reminiscent of a stylized peg or hook, anchored two distinct phonetic roles. Over time, scribal conventions and medieval script developments led to the eventual splitting of vowel and consonant uses (Crystal, 2003):

1. "U": Curved variant used increasingly for the vowel /u/.

2. "V": Retained the pointed form for consonantal /v/.

3. "W": A doubling of "V" (or "u") to represent /w/ in Germanic languages, emerging as "double-u."

4. "Y": Reintroduced from Greek **Upsilon** (Y, υ) – also historically tied to *Waw* – for certain vowel or semi-vowel contexts, especially in Latin transliteration of Greek words (Sampson, 1985).

2.3 English Divergences: U, V, W, Y

In English, the final outcome is that a single Phoenician glyph – *Waw* – yielded four distinct letters:

1. U: A vowel symbol, typically /uː/, /ʊ/, or /ʌ/ in various contexts, also used for /juː/.

2. V: A consonant symbol, representing /v/.

3. W: Another consonant symbol, representing /w/ (absent in classical Latin), introduced for Germanic tongues.

4. **Y**: Operating as a vowel or semi-vowel (/j/, /ɪ/, /aɪ/), historically re-imported from Greek upsilon but genealogically linked back to the same Phoenician root (Cross, 1980).

This divergence exemplifies how alphabet expansions do not necessarily convey new "ontic" references; rather, they reallocate shapes to cover novel phonemic tasks in new linguistic environments (Daniels & Bright, 1996). Today, few English speakers suspect that "W" or "Y" share a deep conceptual link with "U" and "V" – a single "hook/peg" concept from Bronze Age Levantine cultures. The overarching cultural memory of "pegs securing tents" is lost beneath modern orthographic usage. The exoteric user sees these as four separate letters in the 26-letter array, not as genealogical siblings.

2.4 Symbolic Retention

Despite this fragmentation, **U**, **V**, **W**, and **Y** each carry subtle echoes of the same ancient shape. Graphically, "V" and "U" remained close for centuries; "W" is literally "double-u" in name, though it visually approximates "double-v"; and "Y" can appear as a forked variant in certain fonts. Over time, changes in typeface design, printing technology, and orthographic conventions concealed the older unity. Yet a deep genealogical lens reveals them as branches of one tree: *Waw*, the primal peg (Sass, 1988).

3. I, J

Both from "hand/arm" (Yod), diverging in Middle Latin usage.

3.1 Phoenician Yod (𐤉): "Hand" or "Arm"

Where *Waw* denoted a peg, Phoenician **Yod** (𐤉) signified "hand" or "arm." Semitic morphological roots connected *y-d-* with manual functions. The letter was often shown as a pictographic forearm or a stylized hand in the earliest proto-

A Case for Ontolophemes

Sinaitic or proto-Canaanite contexts (Cross, 1980). In purely phonetic terms, Yod served as a consonant /j/ in Phoenician, occasionally modulated for adjacent vowel contexts.

3.2 Greek and Latin Adaptations

When the Greeks adopted Phoenician letters, Yod gave rise to **Iota (I, ι)**, representing the vowel /i/ in Greek. The /j/ consonantal value was less essential in many Greek dialects, so Iota took on a purely vocalic function, eventually adopting simpler shapes for uppercase and lowercase forms (Sampson, 1985). Latin likewise borrowed a variant as **I**, at first bridging both the vowel /i/ and the consonant /j/ (as found in words like "Iulius" /juː.li.ʊs/ or "Ianus" /ja.nʊs/, referencing the Roman god Janus).

Over time, however, Medieval and Early Modern Latin scribes faced the practical challenge of distinguishing the vocalic and consonantal usages:

1. **"I"**: Typically used to mark the vowel /i/ or /ɪ/.

2. **"J"**: Initially a scribal convention – an elongated or tailed "I" at word-initial or consonantal positions. By the Renaissance, "J" was recognized in many languages, including English, to represent /dʒ/ or /j/ (Crystal, 2003).

3.3 English Divergence

English orthography eventually **cemented** "J" as a distinct letter for /dʒ/ (in words like *just*, *judge*), though older forms occasionally spelled these words with "I." This shift was not uniform across European languages: some (like Spanish) reallocated the letter "J" for /x/ or /h/ sounds, while Germanic tongues used it for /j/ (as in German *ja*, /ja/). English, influenced by French scribal traditions, used "J" mostly for /dʒ/ or /ʒ/ in loanwords (Daniels & Bright, 1996). Despite these complexities, the core genealogical fact remains: **I** and **J** originate from a single glyph referencing the "hand/arm" (*Yod*). Their modern usage as separate letters results from medieval attempts to clarify phonetic roles in Latin script (Sampson, 1985).

3.4 Echoes of the Hand

Like the "peg" concept behind *Waw*, the **hand** concept behind *Yod* eventually faded from everyday awareness. The letter shapes "I" and "J" appear to modern eyes as wholly different letters, one for a short front vowel (/ɪ/ or /aɪ/) and the other for an affricate (/dʒ/) or semivowel in some languages. The older, deeper association with the arm or hand, however, can still be glimpsed in historical materials:

- Some academic texts highlight that Yod in Hebrew retains the shape of a small stroke, a "hand" metaphorically.
- In older epigraphic finds, the pictographic link to a forearm remains more overt (Cross, 1980).

Modern typographic design further divorces the letter shapes from their proto-iconic roots. Yet a philological vantage confirms that **I** and **J** are genealogical siblings, much like **U, V, W, Y** are a family cluster from *Waw* (Sass, 1988).

Broader Reflections on Genealogical Splits

These case studies illustrate a recurring dynamic: a **singular** Phoenician letter, referencing a tangible object or concept (fish spine, peg, hand), branched out into **multiple** distinct forms across Greek, Etruscan, Latin, and medieval scribal expansions. Over centuries, these expansions were driven by the phonetic and morphological demands of newly adopting languages (Crystal, 2003). As the alphabet spread geographically – leading to Old English, Old High German, French, Spanish, and beyond – scribes frequently introduced or recognized separate letter forms for previously conflated sounds, creating new letters in the exoteric sense but not new "ontic seeds."

A Case for Ontolophemes

Key Observations:

1. **Loss of Original Reference**: None of the modern letters *X*, *U*, *V*, *W*, *Y*, *I*, or *J* overtly references "spine," "peg," or "hand" in common usage. The primal concept is overshadowed by purely phonetic or orthographic tasks.

2. **Orthographic Efficiency vs. Conceptual Unity**: Alphabets adapt to new languages by splitting or merging letters to represent local phonemes efficiently. This fosters a diverse but historically layered set of graphemes, frequently doubling the apparent inventory without introducing fresh cosmic or agrarian references (Daniels & Bright, 1996).

3. **Esoteric Knowledge**: While everyday literacy does not require an understanding of *Samekh*, *Waw*, or *Yod*, scholars, conlangers, or esoteric traditions may resurrect these old associations, seeing "X" as a crossing spine or "W" as a double-peg, and "J" as an outstretched hand. Such re-imaginings can re-enchant letters with symbolic resonance (Haarmann, 1990).

Conclusion

The letters **X, U, V, W, Y**, and **I, J** showcase how a single glyph's historical identity – whether "spine," "peg," or "hand" – split into multiple Roman letters across diverse linguistic contexts. In the process, the original ontic or pictorial meaning vanished from everyday usage, leaving behind purely phonetic placeholders in modern English orthography (Crystal, 2003). Yet genealogical study reopens these lines, reminding us that behind each exoteric letter stands a deeper, almost-forgotten narrative. A single pictograph once meant "fish backbone" or "hand/arm" or "peg." Through expansions and reinterpretations, we now see a cluster of distinct letters in the final 26-letter exoteric arrangement. By unraveling these wires, we step closer to understanding how alphabets, far from monolithic or static, are living tapestries of historical adaptation – carrying vestiges of ancient lifeways and cosmic symbols deep within their shapes and names (Cross, 1980; Sass, 1988).

Hence, these case studies underscore the tension between the **practical** dimension of letters – simply marking phonemes in daily English – and the **ancestral** dimension, wherein each grapheme once participated in a more unified conceptual realm. This tension crystallizes the theme of the **icosikaihexagon** (26 letters) overshadowing a smaller, archetypal list of fundamental objects. While modern users type "X" or "W" with no thought for fish spines or tent pegs, a genealogical vantage reveals the abiding potential for letters to serve as silent witnesses to cultural memory, bridging the ordinary act of spelling and an older cosmic lattice (Daniels & Bright, 1996).

VI. ESOTERIC AND SPIRITUAL DIMENSIONS

A. Spelling as "Spellcraft"

Across diverse civilizations, the act of **spelling** – arranging letters to form words – has often transcended the realm of mundane communication. Instead, it has been treated as a profound ritual, an invocation capable of **shaping reality** or **invoking cosmic forces**. The English verb "to spell" itself reflects older conceptions of language as inherently magical or incantatory. By examining its etymological roots, and then comparing how runes, hieroglyphs, and Kabbalistic letters have been used by scribes and priesthoods throughout history, we uncover how the very process of writing and naming can function as a form of spellcraft. This section explores how the modern concept of "spelling" conceals an esoteric dimension, where letters and words bridge human intention and metaphysical realities, casting the scribe as a "gatekeeper" of power rather than a mere transmitter of speech (Dickins, 2002; Scholem, 1969).

1. Etymology of "To Spell"

1.1 The Hidden Link to Incantation, Calling Forth Reality by Naming It

In everyday English, "to spell" connotes the act of listing out or writing the letters of a word in order. Yet, historically, the word "spell" resonates with deeper associations of **enchantment** or **incantation**. Tracing this connection reveals a **linguistic** and **cultural** journey that links scriptural recitation to the conjuring of reality:

1. Germanic Roots:
    - The Old English verb *spellian* and noun *spell* indicated a "saying," "narration," or "tale," often with connotations of announcing something significant (Bosworth & Toller, 1898). This usage overlapped with the sense of a

"spell" as a discourse, sermon, or set of words believed to hold special potency.

- Middle English inherited *spell*, still referencing both "discourse" and "magic incantation." Over time, the function of "spelling words" in writing coexisted with "casting spells" or "spellbound" meaning enchantment (Crystal, 2003).

2. Magical Connotation:
    - The notion that *spell* could imply an incantatory formula ties to the older belief in "naming power" – that naming an entity could grant dominion or influence over it (Dickins, 2002). In some Indo-European mythologies, uttering the correct name of a deity, spirit, or phenomenon effectively engaged that power.
    - By extension, "to spell" a word was akin to **deliberately calling it forth**, forging a bridge between signifier (letters) and the signified (concept, object, or entity).

3. Later Developments:
    - Printing technology, standardized literacy, and secular education gradually stripped "to spell" of its older esoteric resonance in mainstream usage (Coulmas, 2003). Yet the vestige remains in phrases like "cast a spell," which merges the lexical sense of "spell" with the older magical worldview.
    - In modern English, "spell" can still imply capturing someone's attention wholly or exercising an enchanted influence. Even if colloquial, the connotation underscores how the act of

naming or reciting letters can enthrall or bewitch (Crystal, 2003).

From an etymological standpoint, **"to spell"** is not merely a mechanical listing of letters but a subtle reflection of a time when language was believed to **evoke** the very essence it named – an "incantation" bridging mind, reality, and cosmos. This conceptual link sets the stage for understanding how, across cultures, scribes and priests harnessed the shaping force of letters and words to assert spiritual or magical authority (Dickins, 2002; Scholem, 1969).

1.2 Calling Forth Reality by Naming It

In numerous mythic and religious traditions, the **power of the Word** stands at the heart of **creation narratives**. For instance, in biblical texts, "God said, 'Let there be light,' and there was light" (Genesis 1:3). The idea resonates with older Mesopotamian or Egyptian cosmogonies in which deities utter or write the names of forces and thereby **manifest** them (Manley, 2012). This cosmic principle underlies the idea that language – especially in written or ceremonially spoken form – conjures or reorders reality.

1. Verbal Summoning:
    - The principle of "naming calls forth being" appears in magical practice worldwide: from ancient Greek incantations invoking daimones to African griots "speaking" genealogies into existence, each tradition invests speech or writing with the force to **shape** outcomes (Smith, 2004).
    - The term "spell" retains a memory of these incantations, where reciting "the right words" in the correct sequence is believed to open

doors to spiritual realms or harness astral powers (Haarmann, 1990).

2. Writing as Stabilization:
   - The shift from purely **oral** incantations to **written** formulas enhanced the sense of permanence and extension. If speaking a name could command ephemeral forces, writing it down "sealed" the effect, making it durable across space and time (Dickins, 2002).
   - Scribes or magicians who recorded incantations on papyrus, clay tablets, or stone thus became custodians of those forces. In a sense, "to spell" a magical formula in writing was to **anchor** that power for repeated use, whether to bless a king, protect a tomb, or secure the afterlife.

Hence, the link between everyday spelling and incantation is neither arbitrary nor wholly overshadowed by modern contexts. It is the residue of an older worldview wherein **naming is commanding**, and letters are the building blocks of that cosmic authority (Crystal, 2003).

2. Runes, Hieroglyphs, and Kabbalistic Letters

Having explored how the concept of "spelling" historically aligns with incantation, we now examine three distinct but resonant examples: **Germanic runes**, **Egyptian hieroglyphs**, and **Hebrew Kabbalistic** script traditions. In each case, the scribes or priesthood served as gatekeepers, wielding letters not merely as symbols of language but as channels to cosmic power (Dickins, 2002; Scholem, 1969).

2.1 Role of Scribes/Priesthood as Gatekeepers to Cosmic Power

A Case for Ontolophemes

Throughout history, literacy was often the domain of a small elite – court scribes, temple priests, or specialized rune-carvers – who intermingled bureaucratic tasks (record-keeping, taxation, law) with **ritual or magical** functions. These classes often cultivated an aura of sanctity or secrecy around writing, using it in rites, curses, or protective spells (Manley, 2012). By controlling written knowledge, they also **monopolized** the means of conjuring cosmic forces, effectively becoming intermediaries between the mortal and the divine (Clunies Ross, 1998).

Key Observations:

1. **Esoteric Knowledge**: These scribes or priests frequently underwent rigorous training, not just in letter shapes but in the conceptual or cosmic associations behind them. Whether a runemaster learning each rune's name and potency, an Egyptian priest memorizing hundreds of hieroglyphs with religious significance, or a Kabbalist meditating on Hebrew letter permutations, the mastery of script was a spiritual discipline (Haarmann, 1990).

2. **Material and Spiritual Power**: In many societies, scribes also managed economic and administrative documents, bridging mundane governance with spiritual texts. This dual role reinforced the sense that writing was a conduit to both earthly authority and metaphysical realms (Smith, 2004).

Against this backdrop, **runes**, **hieroglyphs**, and **Kabbalistic letters** exemplify how "spelling" could become "spellcraft" – the textual shaping of reality, governed by those initiated into its mysteries (Dickins, 2002; Scholem, 1969).

2.2 Runes

2.2.1 Incantatory Traditions in the Germanic World

Germanic runic alphabets, such as the **Elder Futhark** (ca. 2nd to 8th centuries CE), exemplify the synergy of writing and magic (Page, 1999). The word *rune* stems from Proto-Germanic *rūnō* ("secret" or "mystery"), indicating from the outset that each letter was more than a mere sign. Archaeological finds – amulets, weapons, stones – often bear short runic inscriptions believed to ensure protection, victory, or healing (Clunies Ross, 1998).

1. Erilaz and Rune-Carvers:

    - In some runic inscriptions, the term *erilaz* appears, possibly meaning "rune-carver" or "runemaster." Such individuals were credited with esoteric knowledge: the ability to shape fate by carving the correct staves in the correct manner. The act of "spelling out" a name or formula was effectively interlacing incantations into wood or stone (Dickins, 2002).

    - This resonates with the older sense of "to spell" as an utterance that conjures. Runes could be recited aloud in a chant-like manner; simultaneously, their carving might "bind" the intention into material form (Haarmann, 1990).

2. Examples of Magical Usage:

    - Rune stones in Scandinavia occasionally carry short curses or protection formulas. The presence of Odin, the god associated with runic knowledge (in the mythic sense that he discovered runes by hanging from the World Tree), further cements the magical aura (Page, 1999).

- Bracteates (thin gold medallions) from the Migration Period sometimes feature runic inscriptions, suggesting an amuletic function, in which naming or referencing certain runic staves was believed to tap into divine or protective energies (Clunies Ross, 1998).

2.2.2 Spellcraft or Wordcraft?

From the vantage of mainstream literacy, runes might seem simply an alphabet for Germanic speech. Yet the incantatory dimension emerges when we see "spelling" as akin to "spellcasting." Each rune's name (e.g., *Fehu*, *Ansuz*, *Tiwaz*) carried a conceptual significance – wealth, divine inspiration, victory. Thus, listing them or carving them in an order was an act of **symbolic summoning**, not just phonetic coding. The line between **writing** and **magic** was blurred, with the scribe acting as an agent who commanded fate through script. In modern contexts, runic revivalists or esoteric practitioners still treat runes as channels for sacred or psychic power (Dickins, 2002).

2.3 Hieroglyphs

2.3.1 The Egyptian Scribe-Priest

Egyptian **hieroglyphs** date back to at least 3200 BCE, forming one of the oldest writing systems in human history (Manley, 2012). While they functioned for administrative or royal inscriptions, hieroglyphs also **symbolized cosmic principles**. Many glyphs were pictorial: an owl for "M," a falcon for the god Horus, a vulture for "A," etc. (Haarmann, 1990). This iconic dimension merged religious significance with textual usage. Egyptian scribes were often affiliated with priesthoods, learning not only how to represent language but also how to preserve the cosmic order (Ma'at) through correct writing:

1. Role of the Temple Scribe:

- Scribes documented offerings, invocations, and dedications. They carved spells on tomb walls ensuring the deceased's journey to the afterlife, furnishing "magical spells" in the form of hieroglyphic texts (Manley, 2012).
- The phrase "to spell a name" could coincide with ensuring that name's existence in the cosmic cycle. By erasing or defacing a pharaoh's name from inscriptions, successors aimed to **obliterate** that pharaoh's afterlife continuity – an inverse incantation (Allen, 2014).

2. Hieroglyphic Magic:
   - Funerary texts (e.g., the Pyramid Texts, Coffin Texts, and Book of the Dead) featured spells that pharaohs or private tomb owners used to navigate the Duat (underworld). Each hieroglyphic line was a coded incantation; reciting or reading them "activated" protective or guiding forces (Manley, 2012).
   - The scribe's role was pivotal. By writing meticulously, they ensured the spells remained efficacious. Mistakes could break the incantation's potency, highlighting how "spelling" in the sense of correct letter usage was indeed "spellcraft" shaping the deceased's destiny (Haarmann, 1990).

2.3.2 Continuity of the Sacred Script

While Egypt eventually adopted Demotic and Greek scripts for administrative tasks, **hieroglyphs** retained a sacred or ceremonial status well into the Ptolemaic and Roman periods. The priesthood's guardianship over hieroglyphic knowledge sustained the belief that certain signs carried direct ties to gods or cosmic events (Allen, 2014). Thus, scribes functioned as **gatekeepers** of cosmic power, their orthographic skill intrinsically linked to theological understanding – a synergy of theology, language, and magic.

2.4 Kabbalistic Letters

2.4.1 Hebrew Alphabet as Divine Blueprint

In **Hebrew** tradition, particularly within **Kabbalah**, each of the 22 consonantal letters is seen as a building block of creation. Texts like the **Sefer Yetzirah** posit that God used these letters to **speak** or **spell** the world into existence (Scholem, 1969). This worldview invests the Hebrew script with a cosmic resonance – far beyond a normal phonetic system:

1. Letters as Pathways:

    - Kabbalists often explore how each letter (Aleph, Beth, Gimel, Daleth, etc.) aligns with aspects of reality – planets, zodiac signs, elements – thus forming a universal schema (Kaplan, 1997). Spelling a word might rearrange these cosmic energies.

    - Some Kabbalistic meditations focus on combining or permuting letter sequences as a form of mystical practice, believing that correct letter manipulations unlock hidden spiritual truths (Scholem, 1969).

2. Scribes and Soferim:

    - Traditional Jewish scribes (*soferim*) who copy Torah scrolls do so under stringent ritual guidelines, believing each letter must be formed precisely, lest the sacred text lose its sanctity. In effect, the act of writing is a liturgical deed – **spelling** the text upholds the cosmic or covenantal order (Haarmann, 1990).

- Kabbalists sometimes highlight the oral chanting or "spelling out" of Hebrew letters in prayers, bridging the sonic dimension with the written. Each letter is thus a node of divine potency that, when combined correctly, forms a "spell" of creation or redemption (Scholem, 1969).

2.4.2 The Confluence of Incantation and Name

Kabbalah exemplifies how naming and writing can converge to "call forth" divine manifestations. Reciting the Tetragrammaton (YHWH) or dissecting it into combinations can be seen as an act of **spellcraft** – the scribe or mystic manipulates letters to approach or unify with the divine (Kaplan, 1997). This resonates with earlier conceptions of "to spell," implying that enumerating or enumerating letters shapes the spiritual environment. The scribe's capacity to inscribe or pronounce letters thus confers a gatekeeping function, bridging ephemeral life with the eternal realm of the Word (Coulmas, 2003).

Synthesizing the Esoteric Dimension

Spelling as spellcraft emerges from the confluence of multiple cultural lines, each asserting that **letters** are not neutral signs but **portals** to cosmic power. Germanic runes, Egyptian hieroglyphs, and Hebrew Kabbalistic script – among many other traditions – demonstrate how scribes and priesthoods historically leveraged the act of writing to **influence** or **mediate** metaphysical realities (Dickins, 2002; Manley, 2012; Scholem, 1969). A few overarching themes:

1. **Naming as Dominion**: Cultures worldwide affirm that naming something can endow the namer with power over it, whether it be a deity, spirit, or cosmic principle. Written letters anchor that power in a tangible medium (Smith, 2004).

2. **Scribes as Initiates**: Those trained to handle these letters become gatekeepers, controlling or guiding the flow of incantatory potential. Societies often venerate or fear these scribes, attributing them with near-magical authority (Clunies Ross, 1998).

3. **Ritual Performance**: The synergy of reading, reciting, chanting, or carving letters invests them with performative efficacy. The difference between a random arrangement of symbols and a "spell" is the ritual context in which the letters are inscribed or pronounced (Coulmas, 2003).

Therefore, while contemporary readers might treat the phrase "to spell a word" as a wholly prosaic function, the deeper historical horizon reveals that **spelling** can be akin to **casting** – a conjuring process entwined with cosmic narratives and esoteric practices.

Conclusion

The **etymology of "to spell"** illuminates how, in older languages, speech acts and writing acts blurred into **incantations**, bridging everyday reality with spiritual domains. Across cultural contexts – be it runic carving, Egyptian hieroglyphic inscriptions, or Kabbalistic letter meditations – **letters** and **naming** have repeatedly been treated as potent instruments of creation, transformation, and cosmic linkage (Dickins, 2002; Scholem, 1969). In each tradition, **scribes** or **priesthoods** functioned as gatekeepers, harnessing script to bless, curse, guide the dead, or even sustain the cosmos.

Despite the secularization of modern literacy – where "spelling" is often taught as an arbitrary skill, divorced from any esoteric resonance – echoes persist in our language. We still speak of "casting a spell," being "spellbound," or "misspelling," faint linguistic footprints of a time when to spell was literally to conjure. Although many letters in modern

English orthography no longer evoke their ancient conceptual moorings, the hidden synergy between **spelling** and **spellcraft** remains available to those who peer beneath the surface. By revisiting runes, hieroglyphs, and Kabbalistic letters, we rediscover a universal phenomenon: writing can be an act of **naming reality into presence**, bridging mortal intention and cosmic design.

Thus, while we primarily rely on alphabets for pragmatic communication, the **esoteric dimension** reminds us that at the core, "letters" are **ontic** seeds that once signified animals, objects, or cosmic forces – each shape a potential channel for magical or spiritual invocation. In exploring this perspective, we not only enrich our understanding of history and philology but also re-inject a sense of **wonder** into the humble act of putting letters together to form words. Indeed, to "spell" might never be merely to "transcribe sound" but to **call forth** a shard of reality, a ritual echo of cosmic creative power that scribes, runemasters, and priestly castes once guarded with reverence (Dickins, 2002; Haarmann, 1990; Scholem, 1969).

B. Persistence of "Fundamental Objects" in the Physical World

Even as ancient scripts have dissolved into the pages of history or become modern alphabets divorced from their original symbols, many of the **fundamental objects** that once animated these letters persist in the physical environments that shaped them. In some cases, the living world endures where entire civilizations have risen and fallen, testifying to the **ecological embedding** of writing systems. This duality is poignantly illustrated by the **Horus hawk** in Egypt – once an icon of a god-king's power, now simply a bird hovering over the same skies the ancients knew – and in countless other instances wherein animals, plants, tools, or geographical features that inspired script signs continue to populate the land. Here, we explore how such tangible realities underscore the **ontic** nature of early letters, highlighting that they were never abstract from the start but grounded in an intimate engagement with everyday or sacred landscapes.

1. The Horus Hawk in Egypt

1.1 The Living Falcon in Giza: Vestiges of a Grand Civilization

In the shadow of the Giza Plateau, towering pyramids and the Sphinx bear silent witness to the grandeur of Ancient Egypt – one of the world's oldest and most iconic civilizations. Yet, while the monuments stand as testaments to human ingenuity, a lesser-noticed continuity lies in the **living falcons** that continue to glide across Egypt's sky. One such falcon species, likely akin to those worshipped in antiquity as the embodiment of **Horus**, symbolizes a **natural continuity** that outlives dynasties (Manley, 2012). In the Old Kingdom and beyond, Horus was depicted as a falcon or falcon-headed man, championing divine kingship and serving as a protector of the pharaoh. The image of Horus as a raptor soared in carved reliefs, sculptures, and hieroglyphic inscriptions, knitting the avian presence into the very fabric of Egyptian cosmology (Allen, 2014).

1. Horus the Falcon-God:
    - Portrayed often perched above cartouches bearing the pharaoh's name or presiding over temple gateways, Horus embodied the synergy of earthly and divine realms. Egyptians revered falcons for their keen eyesight and regal bearing – qualities transposed onto the concept of divine kingship (Manley, 2012).
    - The letter that might have depicted a falcon in hieroglyphs was not purely a phonetic sign but signaled cosmic or theological ideals (Haarmann, 1990). The presence of a falcon glyph in inscriptions could indicate either a sound, a classification (determinative for divinity), or a direct invocation of Horus's guardianship.

2. Contemporary Reality:
    - Today, visitors to Giza might still glimpse falcons or hawks circling overhead in search of prey. Although the complex theology that once deified these birds has faded, the **biological continuity** remains (Manley, 2012). The falcon itself, as an evolving species, outlasts the human empire that wove it into elaborate religious structures.
    - This points to a broader phenomenon: while the scribes and priests who immortalized birds in stone and papyrus are long gone, the **natural reference** they depicted – an actual raptor – continues to thrive, bridging the ancient

symbolic realm and modern ecological reality (Haarmann, 1990).

1.2 Ancient Scripts Referenced Real Animals and Forces

The Egyptian falcon motif exemplifies how ancient scribes drew upon **real animals** and **active forces** in their environment when conceiving letters, signs, or iconography. Hieroglyphs were profoundly pictographic at the start, reflecting the literal presence of animals – crocodiles, vultures, cobras – significant to daily life and spiritual beliefs:

- **Crocodiles** in the Nile delta were deified as Sobek or used as determinatives for reptilian references.
- **Scarabs (dung beetles)** became potent emblems of rebirth and the sun's daily cycle.
- **Hawks or Falcons**, like Horus, soared overhead and were integrated into divine imagery, signifying watchfulness and celestial authority (Allen, 2014).

Through the **mediation** of scribes, each sign in the hieroglyphic script – though eventually stylized – had origins in living creatures or culturally pivotal phenomena (Manley, 2012). Moreover, as these animals persisted beyond the heyday of pharaonic dynasties, their presence underscores how the fundamental objects or beings that once shaped entire cosmic maps remain tangible in the modern landscape. Falcon still hunts near Giza, embodying an **unbroken ecological thread** from millennia past to the present (Haarmann, 1990).

2. Ecological Embedding

2.1 "Ontic Units" Were Not Abstract

From the vantage of historical philology, many ancient scripts – proto-Sinaitic, Phoenician, Egyptian, Sumerian – appear to have begun with **concrete references** to daily life: the **ox** (Aleph), the **house** (Beth), the **camel** (Gimel), the

fish (Nun). Such references remind us that the earliest letters functioned as **ontic units**, each tied to a direct, physically encountered object or concept (Cross, 1980). Over centuries, repeated stylization and adaptation for different languages – like Greek, Latin, or Arabic – eroded the pictographic clarity. The phonetic role overshadowed the older symbolic or ecological link.

Yet the fundamental objects themselves – livestock, dwellings, wild creatures, and daily implements – **did not vanish**. Even as societies advanced, many of these items continued to form the backbone of agrarian, pastoral, or early urban lifestyles. Fields still needed **oxen** for plowing until very recent history. Fish remained a dietary staple for coastal or riverine communities, and water (Mem) forever defined the possibilities of settlement (Daniels & Bright, 1996). That these items endure physically, while the script's conceptual link to them often fades, highlights the tension between ephemeral cultural forms (alphabets, dynasties) and relatively **persistent** ecosystems.

Key Instances:

1. Oxen:
    - Once fundamental to Phoenician "Aleph," the presence of these robust bovines in farmland persisted into modern times. The letter "A," though no longer depicting an ox head, is still traced back to that origin (Sass, 1988).

2. Camels:
    - Represented by "Gimel" in the Semitic script, camels remain integral to certain desert societies, bridging trade routes across North Africa and the Middle East. These animals continue to shape local ecologies, albeit less so in industrialized contexts (Cross, 1980).

A Case for Ontolophemes

3. Fish:

    ○ "Nun," signifying fish, underscores how aquatic life was a mainstay for nourishment. Fisheries in the eastern Mediterranean or along the Nile still flourish, albeit under modern fishing regulations and technologies. The letter's original reference remains physically relevant (DeFrancis, 1989).

Such continuity ensures that even if the script morphs beyond recognition, the **ecological basis** that birthed the sign remains on the land or in the waters. This actual presence stands in silent conversation with the alphabets that once anchored cultural cosmologies in these very objects (Haarmann, 1990).

2.2 Enduring Landscapes and Cultural Memory

Ecological embedding is not merely a matter of "the same animals are still around." It also speaks to how entire **landscapes** – rivers, mountains, deserts – molded the ethos of early writing systems. For example, the prevalence of "house" (Beth), "fence" (Heth), and "door" (Daleth) reflect stable architectural motifs in Levantine dwellings. Even in modern times, rural communities in the Middle East might build houses with analogous structures (mudbrick walls, enclosed courtyards), echoing earlier prototypes (Daniels & Bright, 1996). Meanwhile:

1. Desert Ecosystems:

    ○ Camels or goats remain pivotal in certain nomadic societies. While global modernization has introduced motor vehicles and other technologies, pockets of pastoral life exist, preserving a link to the environment that originally shaped scripts like Phoenician or Aramaic (Cross, 1980).

2. River and Marsh Environments:
    - Fish (Nun) and water (Mem) reflect a widespread reliance on aquatic habitats. The Tigris-Euphrates system shaped Sumerian cuneiform in ways reminiscent of how the Nile shaped Egyptian hieroglyphs. People still fish these rivers, cultivate farmland with irrigation, and worship or respect water as a precious resource. The environment that gave rise to "Mem" endures (Sass, 1988).

By noticing how these **living contexts** persist, we see that the ontic seeds behind letters remain anchored in real-world usage. Houses continue to be built, water remains vital, fish are still caught. The only difference is that modern orthography no longer highlights these references, focusing on the functional arrangement of letters for phonetic representation (DeFrancis, 1989).

2.3 Continuities Despite Civilizational Changes

One might wonder: if the entire socio-political framework of ancient Egypt or the Bronze Age Levant has disappeared, does the presence of hawks, camels, or fish truly matter for scripts? The short answer is yes, as it underscores that the earliest scribes and language inventors were **intensely aware** of their surroundings, gleaning letters from a tangible world. The fact that these referents persist in the environment – long after the scribal classes and their theologies have faded – demonstrates the primal synergy of **language** and **landscape** (Haarmann, 1990). Where the scribes are gone, the hawks remain.

A Case for Ontolophemes

Case in Point:

- Egypt and the Falcon:
  - Although no pharaoh has ruled from Memphis or Thebes in millennia, the falcon's presence in the skies around Giza reminds us that the original impetus for depicting Horus as a raptor was deeply ecological and spiritual. The environment that produced that symbolism has changed, but not entirely. A passerby in modern Cairo can still see a hawk or falcon, bridging the ephemeral empire to a still-living raptor species (Manley, 2012).

- Mesopotamia and Marshlands:
  - Despite modern industrial interventions, the Tigris-Euphrates marshes once supporting archaic cuneiform-using communities continue to host fish and certain forms of marsh-based life. Although the empires of Sumer, Akkad, and Babylon are dust, the animals and waters that shaped the earliest signs remain – albeit under environmental pressures (DeFrancis, 1989).

This dynamic underlines how alphabets, though ephemeral, can memorialize **timeless** aspects of existence. When we encounter "fish," "water," or "falcon" references in ancient scripts, we see not just phonemes but an **ecological vantage**. That vantage is physically verifiable – hence the phrase "ontic unit." Scripts never emerged in a vacuum; they sprang from an interplay of farmland, livestock, wild creatures, or geographical features that remain integral to local ecologies (Cross, 1980).

Icosikaihexagon and Icosihenagon

Relevance for Modern Understanding

By acknowledging that these "fundamental objects" endure physically, we gain a deeper appreciation of how **material life** can shape writing systems. Rather than seeing early scripts as random inventions, we recognize them as **reflections** of a society's direct environment – hence the bird, fish, door, or house icons. This fosters multiple insights:

1. Environmental Consciousness:
    - Re-engaging with the environment that birthed the alphabets can encourage **environmental stewardship**. Noticing that an animal like the falcon shaped entire religious and scriptural traditions might inspire respect for its ongoing conservation.
    - Similarly, seeing water (Mem) as a letter's root underscores humanity's timeless reliance on aquatic resources. Literacy can thus become a lens through which to realize the planet's interconnectedness (DeFrancis, 1989).

2. Cultural and Ecological Memory:
    - The continuity of these animals or landscapes provides a living link to older cultural forms. Tourism in Giza or along the Nile sometimes capitalizes on the "Horus hawk" mystique, bridging ancient and modern attitudes.
    - In other contexts, the presence of the "house" as a universal concept (Beth) reminds us that fundamental architectural forms are grounded in human needs that remain constant across millennia – sleep, shelter, communal identity (Crystal, 2003).

3. Inspiration for Conlang or Revival Efforts:

- Individuals who study or create **constructed languages** often reintroduce ecological references to anchor their scripts in a tangible environment. Observing how ancient alphabets derived from real fauna or flora can spark new designs that similarly embed script in local biodiversity or cultural geography.
- Some revival projects attempt to reclaim older symbolic associations – like linking "A" (Aleph) back to the concept of an ox or farmland strength, thus "resacralizing" literacy for environmental or spiritual ends (Peterson, 2015).

The Broader Ontological Thread

The **persistence** of these fundamental objects reveals a broader **ontological** thread: that alphabets, at their inception, functioned as **miniature ontologies** enumerating key aspects of life in the Bronze Age or earlier. While the scribal classes may have been replaced by modern schooling, and ancient theocracies by nation-states, the **ecological realities** remain in many locales. A **hawk** circles the pyramids, a **camel** caravans across desert roads, and a **fish** flips through the waters of the Nile delta or the Mediterranean shore. Each instance offers a living echo of the cosmic or everyday categories that once fueled entire scripts (Cross, 1980).

Concluding Reflections:

1. Physical Continuity, Cultural Amnesia:
    - Humanity often forgets the deep synergy between letters and environment. The hawk in Giza no longer signifies Horus to most Egyptians, but its presence testifies to the continuum that shaped the glyphic record of the an-

cients. Meanwhile, the letter forms themselves have drifted from pictographic clarity, focusing on phonetic tasks rather than ecological references (Sass, 1988).

2. An Invitation to Rediscover:
    - By re-examining these fundamental objects – animals, dwellings, implements – in the modern world, we can experience a sense of **re-enchantment**. The "ontic units" do not have to remain relics of anthropological or philological research; they can become a living interface between script, environment, and memory.

3. Ongoing Evolution:
    - As climates change, populations shift, and technology advances, some of these creatures or structures might face endangerment or transformation. Yet the principle persists: writing evolves from real contexts, and real contexts endure beyond ephemeral cultures. This interplay fosters a dynamic where letters remain hints of a deeper involvement with the land (Haarmann, 1990).

In sum, the **Horus hawk** near the Giza plateau and myriad other physical referents highlight a fundamental truth: alphabets did not emerge from disembodied intellect but from hands shaped by farmland, herds, wildlife, rivers, and deserts. That many such references still exist in today's environment – long after the scribes who immortalized them have vanished – speaks to an enduring synergy between **script** and **nature**. While modernization can obscure these relationships, they remain discoverable by those who step back to consider that the lines and curves of a letter, once upon a time, intimately mirrored the living, breathing realities of a place on Earth (Cross, 1980; Manley, 2012).

Thus, the living falcon that soars above Giza is more than a curious remnant; it is the **continuing presence** of what ancient scribes revered and harnessed in their hieroglyphs, connecting us tangibly to a distant epoch where letters, gods, and the environment were woven in a single lattice of meaning.

Icosikaihexagon and Icosihenagon

Icosikaihexagon and Icosihenagon

VII. APPLICATIONS AND FUTURE DIRECTIONS

A. Re-enchanting Modern Literacy

The historical lens we have applied to alphabets – from proto-Sinaitic and Phoenician onto Greek, Latin, and ultimately modern English – reveals that the letters we use daily are far more than inert symbols. They are **living relics** of earlier civilizations, each originally referencing a tangible object or cosmic principle. Recognizing that "A" once depicted an ox, that "B" signified a house, or that "W" emerged from a tent peg can radically alter how we approach reading and writing. Instead of viewing alphabets as random or purely phonetic constructs, we begin to see them as **portals** to deep cultural memory and ecological awareness. This recognition sets the stage for new educational paradigms, personal explorations, and creative or spiritual practices. In so doing, we can speak of **re-enchanting modern literacy** – breathing life back into letters that have often been stripped of their older symbolic or cosmic significance.

Below, we examine two key domains where re-enchantment can take root: **Personal and Educational** contexts, where children or learners might gain a richer sense of language's lineage, and **Creative and Spiritual** contexts, where poets, calligraphers, mystics, and conlangers can reactivate the aura of "ontolopheme" ancestry.

1. Personal and Educational

1.1 Teaching Children the Deeper Symbolic Roots Behind Letters

For most students, literacy lessons revolve around matching letters with sounds, practicing spelling, and gradually learning to read. In English-speaking environments, educators often have to address the irregularities of English orthography, leading to an emphasis on memorization and rule-of-thumb patterns (Crystal, 2003). However, interlacing in the **historical and symbolic** backstories of letters can spark fascination – replacing some of the drudgery of rote memorization with a sense of **narrative discovery**. Consider these potential approaches:

1. Mythic Storytelling:
    - Teachers might introduce each letter's ancestral tale, explaining how "A" was once an ox head in Bronze Age scripts (Aleph), how "B" came from a house (Beth), or how "M" represented water (Mem). Coupled with simple illustrations or comparisons (an old stylized shape vs. the modern letter), children come to see the alphabet as a story bridging thousands of years (DeFrancis, 1989).
    - Such storytelling can deepen engagement and curiosity. Instead of inert shapes, letters become friends with personalities – "A" the steadfast ox, "B" the welcoming house, "C" and "G" the camel siblings, etc. This fosters an imaginative dimension that standard phonics lessons seldom achieve.

2. Interactive Lessons:
    - A classroom might post a large chart connecting each modern letter with its Phoenician, Greek, or runic ancestor. Students can trace genealogies and see how a single glyph (e.g., Waw) branched into multiple English letters (U, V, W, Y). This exercise, almost like a family tree, invites learners to perceive letters as living genealogical entities (Sampson, 1985).
    - Hands-on activities might include drawing proto-Sinaitic or Phoenician shapes, discussing the animals or objects they came from, or writing short stories about how an-

cient scribes decided to pick a fish, an ox, or a camel to represent certain sounds. In this way, the "randomness" of spelling recedes, replaced by a sense of historical continuity.

3. Connection to Real Environments:
    - Students can be encouraged to observe the environment around them – for instance, local farms or wildlife – and see if they can identify parallels to the "fundamental objects" once used to shape letters. If they visit a farm and see an **ox**, this might anchor them in the prime root of "A." If they watch birds near a lake, they might reflect on the "hawk/falcon" or "fish" references from older scripts (Cross, 1980).
    - Such bridging fosters an **ecological literacy** inseparable from the language curriculum, reminding learners that letters were born from direct encounters with animals, dwellings, or topographical features.

1.2 Respect for Language and Cultural Memory

Beyond sparking fascination, teaching deeper symbolic roots instills an **awareness** that language is not a static or arbitrary system but the product of thousands of years of cultural evolution (Crystal, 2003). This can imbue learners with:

1. Respect for Diversity:
    - By understanding that English orthography grew from earlier alphabets (Phoenician, Greek, Latin) and that each stage integrated new or existing concepts, students gain perspective on how languages borrow from, enrich, and transform each other.

- They also see how other writing systems – like Chinese characters or Arabic script – underwent parallel journeys, evolving from pictographic or conceptual references. This broadens global awareness and empathy toward linguistic diversity.

2. Empowerment Through Historical Insight:
    - Realizing that each letter has a "secret history" can make literacy feel like a privilege, connecting present-day learners to an ancient lineage of scribes and civilizations.
    - In contexts of heritage languages or communities with repressed linguistic traditions, highlighting these genealogies fosters pride and resilience, reinforcing that language is rooted in communal narratives and not merely a code (Daniels & Bright, 1996).

3. Holistic Cognitive Engagement:
    - A more imaginative approach to spelling – where letters conjure images of animals, objects, or daily life – activates multiple cognitive pathways. Studies suggest that visual, narrative, and symbolic elements in language teaching can improve memory retention and deepen conceptual understanding (Zakaluk & Samuels, 1988). Thus, re-enchanting literacy is not only aesthetically appealing but academically beneficial.

2. Creative and Spiritual

While re-enchantment in a formal educational context can revolutionize how children learn to read and write, **creative** and **spiritual** practitioners stand to gain equally from reclaiming the archaic, conceptual dimension of letters. From poets seeking fresh images to conlangers building new languages, the **"ontolopheme"** ancestry of alphabets offers inexhaustible inspiration. Likewise, mystics or calligraphers can harness the letters' older symbolic resonance to create a **sacred script** bridging inner and outer worlds.

2.1 Poets, Calligraphers, and Mystics

2.1.1 Poetic Imagery

Poets frequently rely on the **evocative power** of language. Recognizing that "B" used to symbolize a "house" can lead to metaphors or images that recast the letter's shape as a refuge, an enclosure, or a threshold. Similarly, re-centering "M" as "water" might prompt poems that dwell on the fluid, rolling nature of the /m/ sound, forging an **iconic synergy** between phonetics and semantics (Crystal, 2003). By delving into archaic meanings, poets can reawaken what Seamus Heaney once called the "word-hoard" – a sense that words are ancient keys to storied depths of culture.

1. Concrete Poetry and Visual Arts:
   - In **concrete poetry**, letter shapes themselves become integral to the poem's structure. Understanding the older forms (like Phoenician Aleph or the runic Fehu) can add layers of meaning. A poet might embed these forms in the layout, evoking the original conceptual references (Dickins, 2002).
   - **Calligraphers** exploring multiple scripts – Latin, runic, or even faux-Phoenician designs – can experiment with shapes that hint at older pictographs (e.g., stylized horns for "A," waves for "M"). This approach ties visual artistry back to the letter's primal significance.

2. Mystical Practices:

- As explored in traditions like Kabbalah, writing can be a mystical practice: each letter becomes a portal to cosmic energies (Scholem, 1969). Beyond Hebrew letters, individuals might reinterpret Latin letters in a similar mystical vein, recalling that "U, V, W, and Y" all spring from the "peg" symbol Waw, linking them to ideas of support or bridging.

- Ritual or esoteric groups might design meditations around reciting letters in a way that conjures their archaic sense – "I greet the house, the fish, the ox, the hand" – turning the act of "spelling out loud" into a ceremonial invocation of cosmic or elemental forces. This can add depth to spiritual rites, forging a conscious link between mundane literacy and higher symbolism (Dickins, 2002).

2.2 Conlangers and Script Designers

Perhaps the most fertile domain for re-enchantment is **constructed languages (conlangs)** – a realm where enthusiasts or professionals (like Tolkien or modern language creators) purposely design new alphabets or grammar systems that embed cultural or mythical significance (Peterson, 2015). By drawing on the principle that older letters were once **ontolophemes** – encoded references to animals, architecture, body parts, and cosmic energies – conlangers can:

1. Design Alphabets Rooted in Real or Imagined Environments:

    - A conlang might ground each letter in local flora, fauna, or geography, paralleling how Phoenician scribes used "ox," "house," or "fish." This approach fosters a living synergy between the language and its fictional or real

A Case for Ontolophemes

   setting, re-creating the archaic synergy of script and environment (Sass, 1988).

   ○ The result is an internally coherent writing system where readers sense that each glyph is "alive" with meaning, not arbitrarily shaped. This can yield deeper immersion for fantasy realms or creative universes, reminiscent of how Tolkien's Tengwar and Cirth scripts integrated linguistic form with Elvish or Dwarven culture (Dickins, 2002).

2. Reclaim Symbolic or Magical Functions:

   ○ Conlang creators might incorporate symbolic or magical features into their scripts, specifying that writing certain letters in certain sequences channels "energy" or "luck." This directly echoes the runic idea of a **bind-rune** or the Kabbalistic notion of letter permutations for mystical effect (Scholem, 1969).

   ○ By re-enchanting letters with conceptual weight – say, "Fehu" stands for wealth, "Ansuz" for divine breath – authors can replicate the ancient dynamic where "spelling" was "spellcasting." The script becomes a story in itself, forging a meta-layer of lore that engages players in role-playing games, readers of fantasy novels, or immersive conworld participants.

3. Bridging Past and Present:

   ○ Another angle is to craft partial "revivals" of archaic scripts, bridging modern orthographic needs with older symbolic forms. For instance, a conlanger might adapt Phoenician letters to represent a reimagined language, ensuring each letter still references the environment but in a modern ecological or sociopolitical setting. This synergy fosters a **creative anachronism** that reaffirms the fundamental principle: alphabets can be living testaments to cultural relationships with the land and cosmos (Sampson, 1985).

Toward a Re-enchanted Literacy

From the vantage of these two domains – **personal/educational** and **creative/spiritual** – re-enchanting literacy emerges as a multi-layered project. On the one hand, it seeks to **reconnect** each letter with its genealogical or conceptual **seed**, demonstrating that what we call "A," "B," or "C" are not random but trace back to the very real and historically significant objects that shaped them. On the other hand, it fosters an environment where learners, writers, and creative spirits can use letters to **invoke** wonder, forging stronger ties with cultural memory or ecological realities.

Key Prospects for the Future:

1. Curricular Innovation:
    - Schools might integrate short "histories of letters" modules in reading curricula, using modern technology – like interactive apps or VR experiences – to show each letter's transformation from archaic pictograph to present form. This can reduce tedium, enhance memorization, and cultivate respect for the cultural lattice behind scripts (Crystal, 2003).

2. Public Exhibitions and Museums:
    - Museums or cultural centers can host interactive exhibits demonstrating the genealogies of alphabets. Imagine standing in a gallery that visually morphs "Aleph" from an ox drawing

into "A" in a swirl of shapes. Coupling it with physical artifacts (ox skulls, house plans, or actual falcon exhibits) anchors the intangible script in tangible reality.

3. Revival Movements:
    ◦ In some communities, re-enchantment might align with cultural revival efforts – perhaps indigenous or minority groups reclaim older orthographic forms or symbolic scripts, reviving the synergy with land and tradition. Such movements underscore that "letters" can be instruments of identity and decolonization, not just rhetorical devices (Daniels & Bright, 1996).

4. Conlang Breakthroughs:
    ◦ Contemporary conlangers or creative authors may produce alphabets that intentionally embed environment-based references. This can evolve into new forms of interactive literature or multimedia experiences, where readers learn the script by exploring a fictional ecosystem, each letter resonating with its ecological or mythical impetus.

In totality, re-enchanting modern literacy acknowledges that while alphabets have become standardized, de-spiritualized, and widely taught for functional purposes, their ancient roots remain **accessible** – and tapping those roots can transform reading from a mechanical skill to an aesthetically and spiritually **fulfilling** endeavor (DeFrancis, 1989). By reminding ourselves and our children that these letters once stood for livestock, dwellings, fish, and cosmic objects, we awaken a sense of **grandeur** that can rekindle curiosity, empathy, and creativity in the realm of language.

Concluding Reflections

As we stand in a rapidly digitizing age, where texting, tweets, and AI-driven language models accelerate communication flows, it might appear that **alphabetic letters** are more standardized and prosaic than ever. Yet precisely in such a context, the impetus to **re-enchant** arises: exploring letters as **"ontolophemes"** that once signified vital objects and cosmic energies. This approach does not require discarding modern functional literacy; instead, it extends and deepens it, interlacing narrative, ecology, and spirituality into the act of reading and writing.

1. **Personal Fulfillment**: For children or adult learners, tracing the hidden story of a letter can spark awe – reminding them that language is a living bridge between mind, environment, and social memory.

2. **Cultural Enrichment**: By retrieving the genealogies of alphabets, communities can cultivate deeper identity, bridging ancient traditions with contemporary voices.

3. **Artistic and Spiritual Renaissance**: Poets, conlangers, and mystics can harness these genealogies, forging new forms of expression that echo the older synergy of incantation, cosmic design, and everyday life.

4. **Sustainable Literacy**: Recognizing alphabets' ecological anchors can prompt reflection on how language shapes our relationship with nature. Perhaps the "house" or "ox" once animating letters can rekindle contemporary stewardship for farmland, wildlife, or water.

Ultimately, **re-enchanting modern literacy** is not a nostalgic retreat into the past, but a forward-looking endeavor that harnesses the best of scholarship, pedagogy, and creative innovation. It challenges us to see that the so-called

A Case for Ontolophemes

"random letters" we type or trace every day harbor the ghosts of fish and falcons, stables and wells. Embracing that revelation can restore wonder to the simplest acts of spelling, turning each line or curve of a letter into an echo of life's abiding mysteries.

In that spirit, tomorrow's reading lessons – and tomorrow's poems, scripts, or spiritual chants – might transcend the mechanical. They may unify function and reverence, bridging the technical with the cosmic, and thus fulfilling the alphabets' earliest promise: to be a **reflection** of the world's living essence etched into visual forms, forging a dialogue between mind, matter, and the intangible realms that once danced in the hearts of ancient scribes.

B. Conlang Design and "Ontic Alphabets"

The modern revival of linguistic creativity and the widespread adoption of **constructed languages (conlangs)** – whether for literature, film, gaming, or personal artistic expression – has reinvigorated questions about the nature and purpose of writing systems. While many conlang scripts follow a utilitarian path (assigning glyphs to phonemes in a straightforward manner), an increasing number of conlangers seek something richer: an **ontic alphabet** that references a local environment, cosmology, or cultural worldview in every stroke. By doing so, they echo the archaic synergy observed in ancient Semitic scripts, runes, hieroglyphs, or other pictographically grounded systems, wherein each glyph was more than a letter; it was an **ontolopheme** – a symbolic seed bridging ecological objects and cosmic forces with phonetic function.

Below, we outline two major avenues for integrating these deeper symbolic dimensions into a conlang's writing system: crafting **new sacred scripts** that consciously reference an environment or cosmology, and developing **phonosemantic symbolism**, melding phonetic utility with shapes that evoke the script's cultural or mythical bedrock.

1. New Sacred Scripts

When conlangers or creative writers talk of a "sacred" script, they typically mean a writing system that does more than capture speech sounds. It also codifies a belief system, a pantheon, or an ethos – imprinting each glyph with spiritual resonance. Such scripts often appear in fantasy literature (e.g., Tolkien's Tengwar, which merges aesthetic grace with Elvish lore) but can also arise in real-life cultural revivals or spiritual movements seeking to anchor language in **local en-**

vironment or **cosmology** (Peterson, 2015). The fundamental notion is to **purposely** embed ecological, mythic, or ritual significance into each letter, replicating the synergy we see in the earliest alphabets, runic staves, or hieroglyphic ideograms.

1.1 How to Craft an Alphabet from Scratch that Consciously References Local Environment or Cosmology

1.1.1 Establishing a Thematic Foundation

- **Identify the Cultural/Spiritual Milieu**:
  Before drawing shapes, define the cultural or religious backdrop of your conlang. Who are the people or beings using this script? Do they worship sky gods, venerate specific animals, or revolve around elemental forces? If your conlang belongs to an imaginary desert society, consider how the scarcity of water, reliance on camels, or fear of sandstorms might shape symbolic references (Dickins, 2002; Haarmann, 1990).

- **List Fundamental Objects or Concepts**:
  Much like Bronze Age Levantine scribes singled out "ox," "house," "door," or "fish," decide on 15–25 prime realities crucial to your fictional or revived culture: local fauna, revered minerals, forms of weather, cardinal deities. These become **ontic seeds**, each signifying a concept that will be woven into the script (Cross, 1980).

1.1.2 Pictorial or Abstract Roots

- **Choose a Base Aesthetic**:
  Will your script start with **pictographic** forms – each glyph resembling the object it denotes – or **geometric** shapes that hint at the concept symbolically? For a mountainous culture, letters might revolve around triangular motifs (mountain peaks); for a sea-faring

one, they might flow with wave-like curves (Peterson, 2015).

- **Bridge to Phonetic Values**:
  Once you have a conceptual or pictorial form for each fundamental object, adapt them to represent the phonemes of your conlang. This might echo the **acrophonic principle** used by early Semites: the first sound of the object's name determines the letter's phonemic value. For example, if your society's word for "falcon" is /fála/, then the letter depicting a falcon might correspond to /f/ (DeFrancis, 1989).

1.1.3 Sacred or Ritualistic Deployment

- **Inscribe Cultural Use-Cases**:
  Decide how your conlang's society uses the script for ritual. Are certain letters only carved on temple walls or used in funeral rites? Are "curse letters" taboo in everyday inscriptions? This invests the script with social-linguistic power, reminiscent of runic or Egyptian practices (Clunies Ross, 1998).

- **Color, Material, and Context**:
  A script's aura can also stem from how it's written – e.g., in red ink for protective spells, or on stone steles for permanent dedications. Pair each letter's conceptual root with mediums or contexts that reinforce its meaning, linking **sacred usage** to the daily life of your fictional or spiritual culture (Haarmann, 1990).

1.1.4 Bridging to Mundane Usage

- **Dialectical or Dual Scripts**:
  In some fantasy or revival scenarios, you might introduce a **dual** script system: a "sacred" one that preserves pictorial references, used for religious or magical texts, and a simplified "public" script for commerce or day-to-day transactions. This echoes how ancient Egyptians balanced hieratic/demotic with hi-

eroglyphs, or how runic usage varied between formal stelae and ephemeral carvings (Sampson, 1985).

- **Ensuring Phonetic Clarity**:
  While symbolic depth is paramount, maintaining a consistent mapping from glyph to phoneme or syllable is crucial if users are actually to read the script. Early alphabets gained traction largely for their efficiency in capturing spoken language, so your conlang's script must also balance symbolic allure with functional viability (Peterson, 2015).

2. Phonosemantic Symbolism

The term **phonosemantics** refers to the interplay where a letter or sound not only encodes phonetic data but also conveys **semantic or conceptual** cues – either via shape, embedded references, or the psychoacoustic qualities of particular sounds. Ancient scripts like runes or hieroglyphs did this naturally: each symbol had a name and conceptual domain, even as it served phonetic roles (Dickins, 2002). Reviving this tradition can endow a conlang script with **multi-layered meaning**.

2.1 Melding Phonetic Function with Inherent Symbolic Shapes

2.1.1 Reminiscent of Runes, Hieroglyphs, or Other Iconic Systems

- **Runes**:
  Each rune in Elder Futhark had a name (Fehu, Uruz, Thurisaz), a phonetic value (/f/, /u/, /θ/), and a conceptual dimension (wealth, strength, giant/thorn). This triple relationship meant the act of "spelling" was also an act of interlacing runic energies. For conlangers, forging a new script can replicate this: name each letter, define its phoneme, and articulate an ar-

chetypal meaning tied to the culture (Clunies Ross, 1998).

- **Hieroglyphs**:
  Egyptians layered phonetic usage (rebuses, acrophony) with semantic determinatives and artistic depiction of real-world elements (Haarmann, 1990). A conlang script might adopt a similar approach, designating certain glyphs as **logograms** or **semagrams** that carry direct meaning, while others handle phonetic tasks.

2.1.2 Systematic Phonosemantic Mapping

- **Align Sound Groups with Thematic Clusters**:
  For instance, all letters that represent guttural or throaty sounds might visually reference cave-dwelling creatures or subterranean myths in your fictional culture. High front vowels might link to airy motifs (birds, wind, sky). This approach orchestrates a conceptual resonance: reading certain words out loud conjures mental imagery tied to the script's shape and meaning (DeFrancis, 1989).

- **Color and Ornamentation**:
  In advanced conlang designs, scribes might mark morphological categories or conjure certain symbolic features (like "divine" vs. "mundane" words) with color-coded or ornamental embellishments. This replicates the multi-level semantic layering found in some ritual scripts, broadening the script's expressive range beyond pure phonetics (Peterson, 2015).

2.1.3 Encouraging Cultural Engagement

- **In-World Lore**:
  If your conlang belongs to a fantasy or fictional setting, you can integrate "mythical origin stories" for each letter or shape, akin to how runic myths attribute the discovery of runes to Odin's sacrifice. This trans-

forms the script from a static code into a living lattice of stories that fictional inhabitants revere or reference (Dickins, 2002).

- **Ritual or Magical Usage**:
By design, some letter combinations might be restricted to priestly incantations or considered taboo in everyday writing, effectively building in the notion of **spellcraft**. This fosters an immersive conworld where "spelling" certain words or combining particular symbols equates to a coded ritual action, bridging language and cosmic power (Scholem, 1969).

2.2 Balancing Aesthetic, Function, and Lore

While phonosemantic symbolism holds immense creative potential, conlangers often grapple with **balancing** the system's elegance and comprehensibility. Ancient scripts like cuneiform or Mayan glyphs were beautiful and multi-layered but sometimes cumbersome to learn due to their complexity (Daniels & Bright, 1996). Modern creators can adopt certain design principles to ensure usability:

1. Gradual Abstraction:
    - Start with a pictographic base but incrementally stylize or simplify shapes so they remain recognizable yet not overly detailed. This keeps writing feasible at various scales and mediums.
    - For instance, a "sun" glyph can become a circle with stylized rays, retaining enough symbolic clarity to evoke the star's significance, while not requiring painstaking artistry for each usage (Peterson, 2015).
2. Tiered Symbolism:

- Some creators design scripts with **primary phonetic** strokes plus **secondary** diacritics or flourishes that embed symbolic references. Hence, an expert can read multiple layers at once – sound, morphological category, and cosmic association – while novices can ignore the extras if they simply need phonetic clarity. This approach parallels how **hieratic** or **demotic** could omit certain pictorial details while still referencing the older hieroglyphic forms in sacred contexts (Sampson, 1985).

3. Synchronic and Diachronic Variants:
   - Within the conlang's fictional history, you might depict an older or "classic" script form replete with pictorial complexity, then introduce a later "reformed" script that retains symbolic hints but is more streamlined for everyday use. The coexistence of archaic vs. modern variants breathes narrative depth into the conlang's cultural evolution (Dickins, 2002).

Conclusion: The Interplay of Culture, Cosmos, and Letters

The aspiration to build "ontic alphabets" in conlangs – where each glyph references an environment, deity, or central myth – mirrors the **original** impetus behind writing systems like those of the Bronze Age Levant, runic Scandinavia, or ancient Egypt. Whether by forging a new sacred script that ties each shape to local fauna or cosmic principles, or by employing phonosemantic symbolism that resonates with archaic traditions, creators reinstate the **lived** and **mythic** dimensions of script. In effect, conlang design steps into a lineage bridging scribes, priesthoods, runemasters, and Kabbalists, each stewarding letters as vessels for cosmic or cultural forces (Scholem, 1969; Clunies Ross, 1998).

This practice does more than pay homage to archaic scripts; it encourages conlangers to reflect on how language truly emerges from human **ecology and spirituality**. By revisiting the interplay between shape, meaning, and sound, they open gateways for fresh linguistic worlds, each letter a symbolic **seed** that can bud into narratives, rituals, or imaginative expansions. Whether these conlang alphabets remain personal art projects, flourish in online communities, or grace the pages of bestselling fantasy novels, they carry forward the ancient principle that an alphabet is not merely a convenient code – it can be a **microcosm** of the environment and cosmology that birthed it (Peterson, 2015).

Practical Reflections:

1. Gather Inspiration from Real-World Ecologies:
    - Before designing a letter set, immerse yourself in the fauna, flora, climate, or belief systems that define your fictional or real setting. Write notes on how each element might double as a conceptual root.

2. Sketch Pictographs:
    - Even if you plan a more abstract final script, start with simple sketches of objects or forces that are central to the conlang's worldview. Gradually simplify these into manageable glyphs.

3. Forge Cultural Myths:
    - Tie each glyph to a short mythic explanation – like an origin story for how the tribe discovered the "camel letter" or the "river letter." These narratives will give internal consistency to your script.

4. Decide on Orthographic Complexity:
    - Are you aiming for a script that novices can pick up quickly, or a richly layered system requiring deeper study? Make choices that match your conlang's social and narrative context.
5. Iterate and Refine:
    - Historical scripts often accrued modifications over centuries. Simulate that process in microcosm: design an archaic form, then modernize it to see how letters might lose or maintain their symbolic force.

By integrating these elements, conlangers continue a practice as old as writing itself: interlacing the **external** environment and **internal** mythic imagination into the glyphs we use to convey speech. The resulting "ontic alphabets" can captivate hearts and minds, just as ancient runes, hieroglyphs, and Phoenician letters captivated – and still captivate – scholars, mystics, and everyday practitioners who sense the deeper significance behind each line and curve. For creative authors, game developers, or cultural revivalists, the possibilities are enormous. Each letter, carefully wrought, can stand as an emblem of a living cosmos, a microcosm of the environment or pantheon, echoing the primordial synergy that once made alphabets veritable **gateways** to reality itself (Haarmann, 1990).

C. Digital Age and AI "Spelling"

1. High-Speed Spellcraft
Language models (like ChatGPT) produce text swiftly – yet rely on the same 26 letters.

In today's interconnected world, we often marvel at the sheer speed and volume of text produced in digital spaces – an environment in which artificial intelligence (AI) systems play a pivotal role. **Language models** such as ChatGPT, GPT-4, and other transformer-based architectures can generate thousands of words in seconds, responding to queries, producing short stories, composing emails, or summarizing complex documents. Despite these advanced capabilities, these models fundamentally rest on the same **alphabetic bedrock** that has evolved over millennia: the 26-letter exoteric English array (or an extended set, in the case of multilingual or specialized models). Thus, the apparent futuristic spellcraft – instant text generation – still depends on letters that trace their genealogy to the Bronze Age Levant, Greek, and Latin expansions (Crystal, 2003; Daniels & Bright, 1996).

Though we see AI-driven systems as "digital wizards" conjuring words from the ether, they rely on computational processes that encode language as sequences of tokens or characters. At root, these tokens are permutations and rearrangements of familiar alphabets, shaped by **historical orthography** that developed in starkly different, often agrarian, contexts. The incongruity of hyper-accelerated digital language generation – capable of producing entire essays in milliseconds – coexisting with archaic script genealogies underscores how deeply the legacy of "ox," "house," and "door" (Aleph, Beth, Daleth) has lodged itself into modern textual infrastructure (Cross, 1980).

Icosikaihexagon and Icosihenagon

1.1 The AI Pipeline and Alphabetic Constraints

To better appreciate the synergy, consider the pipeline behind a large language model:

1. Tokenization:

   o Before the model generates text, input is typically segmented into tokens – subword units that often align with morphological or orthographic boundaries. English-based language models rely heavily on the standard alphabet (plus some additional symbols) to parse text. Even if advanced tokenizers handle multi-byte characters (for emoji, non-Latin scripts, etc.), the core chunking for English remains tethered to the 26 letters, spaces, punctuation, and common letter combinations (Sennrich et al., 2016).

2. Neural Computation:

   o The model uses massive neural architectures (transformers), which learn statistical patterns of word usage and grammar from enormous corpora. Yet these patterns ultimately revolve around tokens that are expansions or permutations of the Roman letters – a script genealogically derived from the older "ox, house, camel" matrix (Sampson, 1985). No matter how sophisticated the internal representation becomes, the final output is shaped to re-assemble letter sequences that adhere to English orthographic norms (unless the model is generating text in other languages).

3. Text Generation:

   o When asked to produce text (like this essay), the model predicts letter sequences (in token form) that form coherent sentences. The "alphabetic environment" remains the foundation, even if overshadowed by billions of parameters and advanced sequence modeling. The legacy of a single Phoenician glyph – like Waw (𐤅) – branching into multiple English letters (U, V, W, Y) remains a hidden but necessary substrate for the final text output (Sass, 1988).

The result is what we might call high-speed "spellcraft": a computational engine producing text at rates no human scribe could match, but still reliant on a historically derived script. In that sense, AI systems exemplify an **ultra-modern** harnessing of an **ultra-ancient** invention: the alphabetic principle. The speed does not negate the genealogical depth. Just as medieval scribes once "cast spells" by carefully enumerating letters on parchment, modern language models do so in microseconds – yet the basic building blocks remain the same: lines and curves that once signified an ox or a fish. The ephemeral illusions of magic, here, are powered by a synergy of advanced mathematics and archaic orthographic heritage (Daniels & Bright, 1996).

1.2 Contrasts and Continuities

While the speed, scale, and global connectivity of AI-driven text generation differ radically from ancient scribal contexts, the **alphabetic continuity** remains. One might highlight several telling contrasts and continuities:

1. Contrast: Scale and Volume
    - A single scribe in Old Kingdom Egypt or Bronze Age Ugarit might produce a handful of inscribed tablets or papyri in a month. A large language model can generate the textual equivalent of entire libraries in that time, re-

sponding to global users simultaneously (Coulmas, 2003). Yet all this text is still pinned to the same conceptual graphemes that once formed the bedrock of religious or agrarian references (Cross, 1980).

2. Continuity: Alphabetic Core

   - Despite modern expansions (such as diacriticals or Unicode symbols), the central 26 letters for English remain the prime channel for textual throughput. Even emoji-based or symbolic expansions do not supplant the Roman script for coherent discourse, especially in professional, academic, or formal communications (Crystal, 2003).

3. Contrast: Mechanization vs. Artisanry

   - Ancient scribes meticulously formed each glyph with stylus or chisel, investing hours of labor. AI "scribes" emit text with zero physical contact, rewriting themselves in ephemeral digital spaces. Yet ironically, both are guided by the same arrangement of graphemic categories – "A" to "Z" – albeit for drastically different social and functional contexts (Sampson, 1985).

4. Continuity: Affirmation of Orthographic Inheritance

   - Because modern orthography (and thereby tokenization schemas) is historically layered, AI must learn the same irregularities, letter merges, duplications, and morphological complexities we do. Whether /k/ is spelled with "C" or "K," or why "PH" can represent /f/, are anomalies that large language models memorize from corpora, just as humans memorize in school (Carney, 1994).

In short, while the pace and extent of AI-based text generation surpass anything the ancients could imagine, the **alphabet** itself remains a stable hinge bridging past and present. If early scribes once believed that "spelling" had an incantatory dimension, modern AI arguably literalizes that notion: a user types a prompt, and an avalanche of text emerges as if conjured from the ether. Yet it all recasts ancient letter shapes in new patterns, reaffirming a continuum of **spellcraft** across epochs (Dickins, 2002).

2. Reviving the Mythic Dimension

Potential for digital mediums to highlight or animate the symbolic lineage behind each grapheme.

Amid this high-speed textual generation, we also find novel opportunities to **rediscover** or **reactivate** the older cosmic or ecological references that once inspired alphabets. Digital mediums – from interactive e-books to augmented reality (AR) applications – can illuminate the genealogical or symbolic dimension of each letter, bridging exoteric usage and ancestral memory. What was once buried in scholarly research can be brought to mainstream literacy experiences, recasting the quotidian act of reading or writing as a moment of **cultural or mythic communion**.

2.1 Interactive and Multimedia Presentations

2.1.1 Animated Script Histories

- **Dynamic Glyph Evolution**:
  Imagine a digital application or museum exhibit where each English letter is displayed in its current form (e.g., "A"), and when users click on it, an animation morphs the letter backward through its historical shapes – Roman "A," Greek "Alpha," Phoenician "Aleph" (𐤀) with an ox-head pictograph – while a

voiceover narrates how that shape once symbolized an **ox** (Cross, 1980).

- **VR or AR Enhancements**:
  Virtual reality systems could let participants "walk through" alphabets, encountering giant 3D letters that shift into their ancestral forms, perhaps accompanied by an audio commentary on how each form ties to agrarian or spiritual references. This immersive storytelling reinvigorates the symbolic lineage that modern orthography mostly ignores (Manley, 2012).

2.1.2 Gamified Learning Tools

- **Child and Adult Literacy Apps**:
  Digital platforms can incorporate genealogical flashcards or mini-games, awarding points to players who link letters with historical objects – "Which letter came from a door shape? Which from an ox?" Instead of memorizing grapheme-sound correspondences purely by repetition, learners discover them via **narrative puzzle-solving**, forging emotional and cognitive connections to each shape's primal meaning (Crystal, 2003).

- **Animated Emblems**:
  An app might show "Mem" (water waves) transforming into modern "M" with a voiceover about rivers, oceans, and the letter's link to fluid motion. Meanwhile, a student spells words using the newly acquired letter, bridging the archaic concept to actual reading tasks. This synergy of mythic imagery and daily usage can spark deeper engagement (Zakaluk & Samuels, 1988).

2.2 AI's Role in Mythic Revival

2.2.1 Automated Script Explanation

Already, large language models can generate genealogical explanations for letters on demand, compiling data from scholarly sources. If integrated into educational software or reading platforms, an AI system could spontaneously illuminate a letter's origin each time a user hovers their cursor – revealing, for instance, that the letter "D" was once "Door" (Daleth). The digital platform might highlight additional context: how "door" symbolized thresholds in Bronze Age Levantine culture, bridging private and communal spaces (Cross, 1980).

2.2.2 Intelligent "Spellcraft" Assistance

One might conceive advanced conlang or orthography design tools powered by AI:

- **Phonosemantic Mapping**:
  For conlangers seeking ontic alphabets, an AI assistant could suggest shapes that reflect local ecology or mythology, translating user-provided sketches into consistent glyph sets. It could cross-reference historical scripts for inspirations – e.g., "If your culture centers on water worship, consider wave-like strokes reminiscent of Mem (מ)."

- **Integrated Mythic Databases**:
  The AI might embed short narratives or archetypal references for each proposed glyph, referencing how ancient scribes assigned meaning to runic staves or cuneiform signs. The conlanger then picks or refines suggestions, forging a script that merges functionality and symbolic depth (Peterson, 2015).

While these capabilities exist in nascent forms, the synergy between AI's generative prowess and the archaic impetus for script design heralds a **renaissance** in literacy, bridging "futuristic" text creation with primeval references to fish spines, tent pegs, and sacred hawks. Computers effectively become modern runemasters, albeit in a secular context, ironically reaffirming that the shapes they generate are anchored in ancient conceptual strata (Dickins, 2002).

2.3 Reconciling Speed with Depth

The digital realm is often criticized for fostering **ephemeral** reading habits – rapid scanning, short attention spans, and superficial engagements with text. Yet reintroducing a mythic dimension to each letter can encourage a deeper, more reflective approach, even if done in small increments:

- **Hyperlinked Letters**:
  Web texts or e-books could hyperlink each letter to a pop-up panel explaining its genealogical significance. While few would click on such links for every letter, the presence of an accessible "letter-lore" resource can invite exploration, especially for those seeking a more meditative reading experience (Daniels & Bright, 1996).

- **E-Calligraphy**:
  Digital stylus applications might incorporate partial "pictographic layering," so each stroke shows a faint ghost image of the old shape. Writers see how cursive "D" merges from a door-shaped archetype or how uppercase "M" echoes water lines. Such e-calligraphy merges the convenience of digital text with the tactile reflection on symbolic heritage (Sampson, 1985).

Thus, even though speed and volume typify digital text output, interactive design can cultivate reflection and wonder. The age of AI does not have to accelerate us away from the primal synergy between letters and environment; it can ironically reveal it, re-embedding alphabets with the cosmic or ecological gravitas they once commanded (Haarmann, 1990).

Conclusion: The Paradox of Modern Spellcraft

In **high-speed AI text generation**, we witness an ultramodern "spellcraft" overshadowing the slow, methodical incantations of archaic scribes. Yet at the core, both rely on letter shapes that reference – and were once shaped by – real-world objects and cosmic principles. The tension between ephemeral digital text production and archaic letter genealogies is not a contradiction, but a testament to the **enduring** power of alphabets, bridging Bronze Age Levant to the intangible domain of neural networks. The same system of lines and curves that emerged from pastoral or agrarian communities is now orchestrated by sophisticated neural architectures to produce near-instant text for global consumption (Crystal, 2003).

Moreover, the **mythic dimension** of these letters – once overshadowed by purely functional orthographic usage – can find new life in digital mediums. Through VR, AR, or AI-driven educational platforms, we can highlight each grapheme's **symbolic lineage**, tying it back to "pegs," "doors," "water," or "fish." This paves the way for a digital literacy that is not solely about efficiency or ephemeral consumption, but about **deep cultural retrieval** – the re-enchantment of reading and writing in the context of advanced technology.

Implications:

1. **Technological**: AI and digital platforms can re-humanize literacy by foregrounding the archaic, ecological, or cosmic origins of our letters.
2. **Educational**: We can design hybrid systems that seamlessly integrate genealogical insights into stan-

dard reading instruction, bridging speed and depth (Daniels & Bright, 1996).

3. **Spiritual/Artistic**: Poets, mystics, conlangers, or visual artists can harness AI to animate the ancient references behind each letter, forging a synergy of "spellcraft" across e-books, interactive installations, or conlang communities.

Ultimately, the digital age's ability to produce **rapid** text at scale may ironically become the best vantage point to reflect on **slow** genealogical truths. AI, with its instant "spelling" capabilities, underscores how alphabets remain stable anchors in a swirling sea of transformation. From archaic scribes penning incantations in temple shadows to ChatGPT responding to global queries, the letters endure – quiet but potent embodiments of "ox," "house," "fish," and "tent peg," sublimated into ubiquitous lines of code. This realization invites a renewed sense of **wonder**: the intangible realm of AI-driven text is built upon the same shapes and lines once carved by runemasters or Egyptian priests for cosmic ends. Thus, even in the lightning-fast present, an archaic hum can be discerned in every keystroke – a hum that beckons us to recover or reanimate the mythic dimension lying dormant beneath modern "spellcraft."

VIII. Conclusion

The previous pages have traced an expansive journey through the **English alphabet** – illuminating its status both as an **exoteric icosikaihexagon** (26 visible letters) and an **esoteric icosihenagon** (21 or so foundational ontic units). Over many chapters, we observed how these dual realities converge in a single script: modern English orthography. On the surface, it is a pragmatic tool with 26 discrete symbols, taught in schools through rote memorization and phonics. Underneath, it hides a deeper lineage anchored in Bronze Age Levantine scripts, each letter once referencing real creatures, objects, or cosmic concepts. This final section interlaces together the main themes, underscores the broader cultural and ecological significance of these letters, and suggests open questions for future explorations – especially relevant at a time when changing environments and technological revolutions invite us to reimagine the role of writing in human life.

1. Synthesis

1.1 Exoteric Icosikaihexagon: 26 Letters in Modern English

On a purely exoteric plane, the **English alphabet** appears as a tidy set of 26 letters: A to Z. Introduced to children with catchy songs, pinned on classroom walls, and employed in countless daily communications, these letters form the immediate facade of modern literacy. They are the "edges" of our icosikaihexagon, each functioning as an apparently discrete sign for one or more phonemes – though, as we have seen, English spelling complicates the straightforward phoneme-letter mapping (Crystal, 2003). Yet this 26-letter system, while stable in visual form, betrays significant expansions and duplications from older scripts:

A Case for Ontolophemes

- **I/J** (both from Yod)
- **U/V/W/Y** (all from Waw)
- **C/G** (both from Gimel)

Where old scripts used one letter to represent a concept and phoneme, we in modern English ended up with multiple letters from the same root. At the exoteric level, no mainstream literacy instruction typically recounts the genealogical merges and splits that shaped "Q," "K," or "X." Instead, each symbol is presumed a distinct entity for spelling words like *queen*, *kite*, or *box*. This results in an outward polygon of 26 sides – a closed array of letters taught as if each had an independent origin (Sampson, 1985; Daniels & Bright, 1996).

Yet the stable front of 26 letters is misleading. Beneath that exoteric shell looms an intricate genealogical web, reflecting historical orthography, expansions from Latin usage, duplications of Phoenician or Greek glyphs, and the interplay of languages across centuries. The exoteric system's familiarity and everyday utility often lull us into forgetting the deeper, older strata that shaped it. We type or scribble these letters with minimal reflection on how "U" once connoted a "peg" or "J" once mirrored a "hand." This tension between **practical function** and **historical complexity** forms the heart of the exoteric icosikaihexagon's story.

1.2 Esoteric Icosihenagon: 21 Root Ontolophemes

By peeling back layers of expansions, we discovered that many of these 26 letters share ancestral glyphs in Phoenician (circa 1000 BCE), which itself derived from earlier Semitic scripts (e.g., Proto-Sinaitic). In that older system – commonly with **22** letters – each glyph corresponded to a **tangible** or **sacred** object, from "Aleph" (ox), "Beth" (house), "Gimel" (camel), "Daleth" (door), "Nun" (fish), "Mem" (water), and so forth. Over time, scribes adapted those shapes and names to Greek, then to Etruscan, then to

Icosikaihexagon and Icosihenagon

Latin. But the conceptual bedrock – **ox, house, fish, door, hand, peg** – informed the script's earliest impetus (Cross, 1980; Sass, 1988).

When we remove the duplications introduced by letter splits in Greek/Latin usage, the system's genealogical core is a simpler **icosihenagon** of about 21 prime references (or 22, if including variants). This older system enumerates the "fundamental objects" of agrarian or pastoral life in the ancient Levant, each glyph an **ontic unit** embodying daily needs and cosmic beliefs (Daniels & Bright, 1996). The "exoteric 26" thus overshadow the "esoteric 21," forging a riddle: how did one letter referencing a "camel" become two letters, "C" and "G," in English? Why do we now treat "U," "V," "W," "Y" as four distinct letters when they once derived from a single Phoenician *Waw*?

Yet the conceptual line between these duplications and real-world references persists. For all the expansions, the ancestral meaning – house, ox, fish, door – lurks behind each modern letter, if only recognized by philological or esoteric inquiry (Crystal, 2003; Haarmann, 1990). In the final analysis, English orthography is a **layered palimpsest**, bridging thousands of years of writing culture. On one side, a set of 26 "edges" forming the icosikaihexagon used in daily life; on the other, a "proto-ontology" of roughly 21 categories shaping an icosihenagon we seldom see, but which gave rise to the shapes and names we still rely upon.

1.3 Continuity of Fundamental Objects Through Millennia

Crucially, these 21 or 22 prime references revolve around fundamental objects that remain relevant. Oxen, fish, birds, water, doors: many remain physically present in the world. A hawk near the Giza pyramids or fish caught along the Mediterranean shore resonates with ancient references to Horus or the letter "Nun." Houses remain cornerstones of domestic life everywhere, while "water" is eternally vital.

A Case for Ontolophemes

This continuity clarifies that alphabets were never abstract from the start – they were shaped by environment and everyday survival. Bronze Age scribes immortalized crucial aspects of their world in glyphs that eventually transformed beyond recognition (DeFrancis, 1989; Sass, 1988).

Such continuity across millennia underscores an **ecological embeddedness** of writing. As old civilizations fade, the real animals and resources endure, bridging ephemeral culture with abiding nature. By acknowledging this bridging, we see that alphabets have always reflected a synergy of **practical function** (capturing speech) and **mythic or environmental** significance (Cross, 1980). Even if modern usage rarely references that synergy, the genealogies show how deeply letters were once entwined with the "stuff" of daily existence.

2. Final Reflections

2.1 Writing as a Potent Mirror of Human Connection to Nature, Culture, and the Cosmos

From archaic runes to modern AI-driven text generation, **writing** remains a dynamic mirror of how humans conceptualize reality. In the earliest alphabets, each glyph's name and shape stood for a force or object that structured agrarian life: cattle for strength and wealth, fish for sustenance, houses for refuge and identity, water for fertility, birds for spiritual watchfulness, and so on (Dickins, 2002; Manley, 2012). Through centuries of expansions and phonetic reassignments, these references receded, but the forms survived. As we discovered, the final arrangement – English's 26 letters – functions well enough for daily usage, yet conceals a **myriad** of genealogical pathways leading back to genuine ecological or cosmic archetypes (Cross, 1980).

Thus, writing is not only a mirror of mental processes or social interactions; it is also a **living index** of humanity's longstanding intimacy with land, fauna, flora, and the cosmos. Each time we form an "A," we unconsciously recall a stylized **ox head** that once symbolized fertility. Each time we read "C," we inherit the "camel" impetus beneath. We can easily ignore these older strata when focusing on immediate communicative tasks – but they remain, a silent testament to the synergy between **culture and environment**.

2.2 Invitation to a Renaissance of Reverence and Creativity in Reading, Writing, and Spelling

Unveiling these onion layers of the alphabet invites new possibilities:

1. Educational Renaissance:
    - Imagine reading curricula or literacy apps that incorporate genealogical flashbacks – showing how "M" was once water lines or how "D" was a door. Instead of seeing spelling as a random code, students might approach it as a storied lattice bridging thousands of years. This fosters respect for language and curiosity about how letters shape thought (Crystal, 2003).

2. Poetic and Spiritual Depth:
    - Poets, calligraphers, mystics, or conlangers can harness the archaic synergy, forging new works that do more than convey meaning. They can re-imbue letters with esoteric, ecological, or mythic forces, bridging the modern and the ancient. Such creative moves can revitalize how we see letters, reminding us that "spelling" was once "spellcasting," an invocation of cosmic or religious energies (Dickins, 2002; Haarmann, 1990).

3. Technological Tools for Cultural Memory:

- With VR, AR, and advanced AI, we can design immersive experiences in which reading and writing become an active journey through symbolic genealogies. The digital realm – often accused of fostering superficial reading – can paradoxically facilitate deeper reflection on the letter's layered significance. By animating each grapheme's older forms or linking them to the environment, we stand at the cusp of a new synergy between technology and tradition (Manley, 2012).

In that light, we see how a "renaissance of reverence" for the alphabet is possible – one that does not hamper everyday communication but elevates it, bridging **efficiency** with **wonder**. The onion layers may remain invisible to many, but for those who look beneath the surface, each typed or penned letter resonates with a hidden cosmic or ecological chord.

3. Open Questions

Having examined the icosikaihexagon (26 letters) and the icosihenagon (21 root ontolophemes), and traced how modern usage obscures these fundamental references, we conclude with broader **open questions**. These inquiries challenge us to reflect on what else might lie concealed in modern scripts and how changing global conditions might spark new forms of writing:

3.1 What Other Hidden or Half-Forgotten "Ontolophemes" Linger in Modern Scripts?

1. Beyond English:
    - English inherits the Roman alphabet, but countless other orthographies exist worldwide – Cyrillic, Arabic, Devanagari, Chinese char-

acters, Korean Hangul, and beyond. Each has genealogical layers, some referencing archaic objects or concepts. For instance, in Devanagari, certain letter forms hint at historical shapes that once had symbolic meaning. Or in Chinese, radicals still preserve references to nature or cultural objects, though many are stylized.

- We might ask: what ephemeral references exist in, say, the letter Ц (Ts) in Cyrillic or the combination of radicals in a Chinese character like 愛 (ài, "love")? Are there half-forgotten ideographic seeds referencing ancient beliefs about emotional states, familial roles, or cosmic energies? Scholars of comparative writing systems may find abundant layers of "ontolophemes" just waiting to be rediscovered (Coulmas, 2003).

2. Minority Languages and Scripts:

    - Indigenous or minority communities often rely on orthographies developed rapidly by missionaries or linguists. Sometimes, these new scripts incorporate external alphabets (Latin, Cyrillic), overshadowing older symbolic traditions. But in other instances, creative adaptations or revitalization efforts embed local environment references. Investigating these newly minted scripts might reveal novel "ontic seeds" that capture present-day ecological or cultural realities.

    - Could there be a script invented in the 20th or 21st century that references solar panels or cell phone towers as fundamental concepts? While seemingly odd, such a move might recapture the archaic impetus: enumerating vital objects of daily life. Perhaps future scripts for newly recognized languages could anchor each glyph in a crucial aspect of the local environment or technology (Daniels & Bright, 1996).

3. Symbolic Reclamation:
    - Even within well-established alphabets, certain letters might harbor hidden genealogical lines not commonly documented. There may be local scripts in parts of Africa, Asia, or the Pacific that merged older pictographs into a modern alphabetic or syllabic system, leaving behind cryptic shapes. Studying them might unearth additional "house," "ox," or "spear" references lurking beneath contemporary usage (Haarmann, 1990).

Thus, the quest to unearth half-forgotten ontic references is not limited to English or the Roman script. The phenomenon is global, reflecting a universal pattern: writing emerges from real-world contexts, and with time, the references fade into standard orthography. Searching for these hidden genealogies across the planet's myriad scripts can reveal further wonders and synergy between environment and orthography.

3.2 How Might Future Alphabets or Conlangs Re-Center Fundamental Objects in Ways That Speak to a Changing Environment?

1. Environmental Shifts:
    - Humanity is now grappling with climate change, mass urbanization, and rapid technology adoption. If alphabets originally captured crucial survival or spiritual references, future

scripts might reflect new ecological or cosmic concerns. Could we see conlangs or real orthographic reforms that revolve around solar energy, endangered species, rising sea levels, or digital connectivity as the "fundamental objects"?

- Instead of "ox" or "door," perhaps a letter might reference "reef" or "wind turbine," signifying the objects that shape modern communities. This would restore writing as a direct mirror of environment, albeit in a drastically altered Earth from that of Bronze Age scribes (Peterson, 2015).

2. Techno-Ecological Synthesis:
   - Some conlang or script creators have begun exploring "post-postmodern alphabets" that deliberately unite new technologies with environmental stewardship. For example, a "cyborg script" might depict microchips or circuit motifs for certain letters, while also embedding references to soil or water cycles for others. By bridging the digital and ecological, these hypothetical alphabets attempt to unify the intangible realm of AI with the tangible realm of planetary life – a synergy reminiscent of archaic writing but adapted to the 21st century (Dickins, 2002).
   - If successful, such alphabets could spur an **awareness** in everyday users that each letter signals a piece of the changing environment – a literal re-centering of fundamental objects that define the modern condition, whether that means "cloud computing" or "coral reefs." In so doing, the script evolves from a mere pho-

netic apparatus to an emblematic register of urgent ecological realities.

3. Adaptive or Dynamic Scripts:

   ○ Another intriguing possibility is the creation of **adaptive** or **dynamic** scripts that morph or reconfigure their shapes in response to real-time environmental data. For instance, an AR-based conlang might shift certain letter forms if local sensors detect rising water levels or changes in air quality. Each letter could reflect the environment's shifting state, echoing older traditions where writing responded intimately to ecological context (Haarmann, 1990).

   ○ While this remains speculative, the principle recasts the original impetus of alphabets – naming crucial objects for daily survival – into a contemporary frame: naming and reflecting crucial *conditions* for planetary survival. If each letter signals an environmental condition, writing itself becomes an ongoing ecological commentary.

Concluding Thoughts on the Future of Alphabets

We stand at a moment where advanced technology (VR, AR, AI) and pressing ecological transformations could re-invigorate the oldest blueprint for writing: **rooting alphabets in fundamental realities**. As the user base for conlangs and creative scripts grows – thanks to online communities, open-source tools, and new media – fresh alphabets might re-center objects or concepts that matter for tomorrow's world. Rather than "ox, house, fish," the script of the future may revolve around "drone, reef, virus," or "cloud server," forging an entirely new set of ontic seeds. Or it might remain archaic in form yet subtly updated with references to global warming, migration, or digital identity (Peterson, 2015).

In either case, the lineage from the Bronze Age remains instructive. We now know how bridging environment, mythic worldview, and phonetic function gave alphabets both durability and cultural resonance. The question is whether we can recapture that synergy intentionally in a modern or future setting, shaping writing systems that resonate with the **contemporary** environment while preserving the timeless sense that each letter stands for something real, something revered, something vital to the community's existence.

Conclusion in Full:

The English alphabet, outwardly a 26-letter grid, is in truth an **icosikaihexagon** overshadowing an older **icosihenagon** of around 21 fundamental references – "objects" that once defined Bronze Age or Iron Age societies. These references – oxen, houses, fish, doors, water, birds, hooks – still exist in the real world, bridging ephemeral cultural epochs with abiding ecological or cosmic realities. From ancient scribes carving runes or hieroglyphs, through medieval expansions and duplications in Greek and Latin usage, to modern AI systems generating text at lightning speed, the same shapes persist, each concealing an archaic synergy between **language and environment** (Cross, 1980; Daniels & Bright, 1996; Sass, 1988).

Unveiling these layers casts writing in a new light, where letters become more than placeholders for phonemes. They become **portals** to older worlds, each stroke thick with memory. This insight can **re-enchant** how we teach, learn, and create language – inviting educators to reveal genealogical stories to students, inviting artists and conlangers to re-inject alphabets with symbolic or spiritual power, and even spurring new technological mediums that highlight each let-

A Case for Ontolophemes

ter's lineage. Far from mere academic trivia, this resurrection of the archaic synergy resonates with deeper impulses in the human psyche: the desire to see words not merely as mechanical codes but as **incantations** bridging mind, nature, and cosmos (Dickins, 2002; Scholem, 1969).

In an era beset by ecological anxieties, cultural fracturing, and digital transformations, alphabets hold quiet but enduring lessons. They remind us that writing – once intimately tied to farmland, cattle, water sources, or cosmic energies – can reclaim that closeness if we so choose. The ephemeral lines of text we fling across screens can become mediums of reflection, bridging the ordinary tasks of reading or emailing with the archaic genealogies that shaped "A," "B," and "C." By exploring or re-centering these fundamental objects, we call forth a future where writing is not only functional but richly **meaningful**, echoing the primal synergy that once made alphabets a **potent mirror** of humankind's connection to **nature, culture, and the cosmos**.

As we conclude, open questions beckon: Are there further "ontic seeds" buried in lesser-known scripts worldwide – signs referencing now-lost animals or geographies? Might future conlangs, crafted for fictional or revived societies, revolve around emergent ecological concerns, forging alphabets that depict coral reefs or solar panels as fundamental references? And ultimately, how might the unstoppable tide of technology – AI text generation, VR-based literacy, or dynamic AR scripts – re-harness the archaic impetus for enumerating the real, the revered, and the cosmic in each letter? In grappling with these questions, we honor the **ever-unfolding** narrative of writing, a lattice that began with fish spines and tent pegs, yet continues to adapt to the changing conditions of our planet and imagination.

Icosikaihexagon and Icosihenagon

APPENDICES

Appendix A: Tables of Letters and Their Phonemes

Table A1: English Alphabet (A–Z) with Common IPA Values

Below is a succinct table illustrating each letter of the **modern English alphabet**, its most frequent or canonical **IPA** (International Phonetic Alphabet) values, and brief **notes** on additional contexts or dialectal variations. Please note that English spelling and pronunciation can vary significantly by dialect; this table provides broad, representative usages.

Letter	Common IPA Value(s)	Notes/Contexts
A	/æ/ (cat), /eɪ/ (name), /ɑː/ (father in many accents), /ɔː/ (law, some dialects), /ə/ (about)	Highly variable. Great Vowel Shift & borrowings contribute to multiple sounds.
B	/b/ (bat)	Generally consistent for /b/. May be silent in words like *lamb* or *doubt*.
C	/k/ (cat), /s/ (city), /tʃ/ (cello, in some loanwords)	Often /k/ before *a, o, u*; /s/ before *e, i, y*. Spelling patterns highly irregular.
D	/d/ (dog)	Fairly consistent. Occasionally silent in words like *Wednesday* (some dialects).
E	/ɛ/ (bed), /iː/ (me, some "-e" final words), /eɪ/ (café, certain loanwords)	Also /ə/ in unstressed positions (e.g., *the*, *taken*).
F	/f/ (fan, off)	Typically stable for /f/.

Icosikaihexagon and Icosihenagon

G	/g/ (go), /dʒ/ (genre in loanwords), occasionally silent (gnome)	Usually /g/ before *a, o, u*; can be /dʒ/ before *e, i, y* (e.g., *gin*).
H	/h/ (hat), silent (hour, honest)	In some accents, /h/ may drop ('erb in some dialects).
I	/ɪ/ (bit), /aɪ/ (site), /i:/ (machine, certain words), /ɪ/ or /ə/ (happily)	Complex due to Great Vowel Shift & loanwords (Italian *piano*, for instance).
J	/dʒ/ (jam, judge)	Derived historically from *I*. /ʒ/ in some loanwords (*garage*).
K	/k/ (kite, back), silent (knight, knee)	Often silent in *kn-* sequences from Old English.
L	/l/ (love, all)	Dark L (/ɫ/) in coda positions for many dialects, occasionally silent (*could*).
M	/m/ (man, seem)	Typically stable.
N	/n/ (not, can)	Can assimilate to /ŋ/ before velars (*bank* /bæŋk/).
O	/ɒ/ (hot in British), /oʊ/ (hope, General American), /ɔ:/ (thought in many dialects), /ə/ (some unstressed)	Highly variable, shaped by historical spelling & dialectal evolution.
P	/p/ (pin, cup)	Silent in some Greek loanwords (*pneumonia*).
Q	/kw/ (queen), occasionally /k/ (conquer, bouquet)	Appears almost always as *qu* in English.
R	/ɹ/ (run, car in rhotic dialects), /r/ in some accents	Non-rhotic accents drop /r/ in coda position (*car* → /kɑ:/ in RP).
S	/s/ (sit, hiss), /z/ (was, dogs), /ʃ/ (sugar, sure)	Often merges to /z/ in plurals or 3rd-person verbs.

A Case for Ontolophemes

T	/t/ (top, cat), sometimes /tʃ/ (nature, partial assimilation)	Flapped /t/ or /d/ in some dialects (e.g., *water*).
U	/uː/ (flute), /ʊ/ (put), /juː/ (use), /ʌ/ (cut)	Greatly influenced by preceding consonants & historical layers.
V	/v/ (van, love)	Not distinct in Old English; introduced from French/Latin.
W	/w/ (win, cow)	"Double-u." Silent in words like *wrap*, *wrist*.
X	/ks/ (box), /gz/ (examine), occasionally /z/ (xylophone)	Reflects Greek or Latin heritage, quite variable.
Y	/j/ (yes), /ɪ/ or /i/ (happy), /aɪ/ (myth in some dialects)	Greek upsilon root. Usage as vowel or semivowel often context-dependent.
Z	/z/ (zoo, buzz)	/ts/ or /dz/ in some borrowed words (*pizza* → /ˈpiːtsə/).

This table captures common phoneme associations in General American or Received Pronunciation–like contexts, acknowledging that English spelling is highly irregular (Crystal, 2003).

Icosikaihexagon and Icosihenagon

Table A2: Phoenician/Proto-Sinaitic Letters with Proposed Symbolic Meanings

Below is a representative set of key Phoenician (or earlier Proto-Sinaitic) letters, their transliterated names, and the often-cited symbolic meanings or real-world objects they referenced. Scholars sometimes debate precise identifications, but these remain widely held interpretations, showing how each glyph once named or depicted a fundamental object, tool, or concept (Cross, 1980; Sass, 1988).

Phoenician / Proto-Sinaitic Glyph	Name (Approx.)	Proposed Symbolic Meaning	Notes on Derivatives / Comments
⌊ / Aleph	Aleph ('ālep)	"Ox," representing strength	Evolved into Greek Alpha (A), Latin A. Ox-head shape likely stylized in earlier forms.
ꟻ / Beth	Beth (bēth)	"House," symbolizing refuge	Greek Beta (B), Latin B. Maintained meaning of dwelling – foundation for domestic life.
⌐ / Gimel	Gimel (gīmel)	"Camel," a key trade beast	G → Greek Gamma (Γ), Latin C (with /k/), then G from modified C. "Camel" bridging desert routes.
◁ / Daleth	Daleth (dālet̠)	"Door," a boundary or portal	Greek Delta (Δ), Latin D. Symbolic threshold between inside/outside, repeated in extended alphabets.
⌐ / He	He (hē)	"Window" or "Breath"	Greek Epsilon (E) in Greek, capturing /e/ vowel. Might reference an opening (window/breath).
⌐ / Waw	Waw (wāw)	"Hook" or "Peg"	Formed basis of U, V, W, Y in later expansions. Crucial for tent-based or building societies.

A Case for Ontolophemes

⁊ / Zayin	Zayin (za-yin)	"Weapon" or "sword"	Greek Zeta (Z), Latin Z. Represented martial or protective power.
目 / Heth	Heth (ḥēṯ)	"Fence" or enclosure	Merged or dropped in Greek and Latin due to pharyngeal /ḥ/ lacking. Symbolic boundary.
⊕ / Teth	Teth (ṭēṯ)	Possibly "wheel" or "basket"	Emphatic /t/ in Semitic. Largely lost in Greek/Latin adaptations.
ʔ / Yod	Yod (yōḏ)	"Hand" or "arm"	Gave rise to Greek Iota (I), Latin I/J. Symbolic of manual dexterity, crafting.
⋎ / Kaph	Kaph (kap)	"Palm (of the hand)"	Greek Kappa (K), Latin K (limited usage), plus interplay with C. Open palm reference in older forms.
∠ / Lamedh	Lamedh (lāmeḏ)	"Goad" or "cattle prod"	Greek Lambda (Λ), Latin L. Represents guiding or prodding livestock.
⁊ / Mem	Mem (mēm)	"Water," wave-like shape	Greek Mu (M), Latin M. Symbolic of chaos or life's source in Semitic myths.
⁊ / Nun	Nun (nūn)	"Fish," sign of sustenance	Greek Nu (N), Latin N. Fisheries crucial for coastal societies.
⟊ / Samekh	Samekh (sāmeḵ)	"Spine," "support," or "fish spine"	Possibly led to Greek Xi (Ξ) /ks/, then Latin X. Symbolic of structural backbone.
O / Ayin	Ayin (ʿayin)	"Eye," vision or awareness	Greek Omicron (O) or Omega (Ω) after repurposing in Greek. Voiced pharyngeal lost in Greek/Latin.
⁊ / Pe	Pe (pē)	"Mouth," crucial for speech	Greek Pi (Π), Latin P. Links writing to orality conceptually.

Icosikaihexagon and Icosihenagon

ϙ / Qoph	Qoph (qōp)	Possibly "monkey," "back of head," or "needle's eye"	Greek Qoppa, Latin Q. Merged usage, generally for /kw/ in English.
٩ / Resh	Resh (rēš)	"Head," leadership	Greek Rho (P), Latin R. Symbolic top or head, critical for morphological expansions.
ᗯ / Shin	Shin (šīn)	"Tooth," devouring power	Greek Sigma (Σ) for /s/, Latin S. Possibly multiple merges with /ʃ/ or /s/ forms.
✝ / Taw	Taw (tāw)	"Mark" or "cross"	Greek Tau (T), Latin T. Basic cross or boundary sign in archaic usage.

Interpretations vary; older shapes might differ. This table highlights each glyph's pictorial meaning and how it eventually shaped Greek, then Latin letters. Some letters merged, dropped, or were repurposed in transitional scripts, reinforcing how each once-living concept dissolved into a purely phonetic role over time.

A Case for Ontolophemes

Appendix B: Visual Charts

(Chart 1: Icosikaihexagon, Icosihenagon, English Graphemes and Phoenician Ontolophemes)

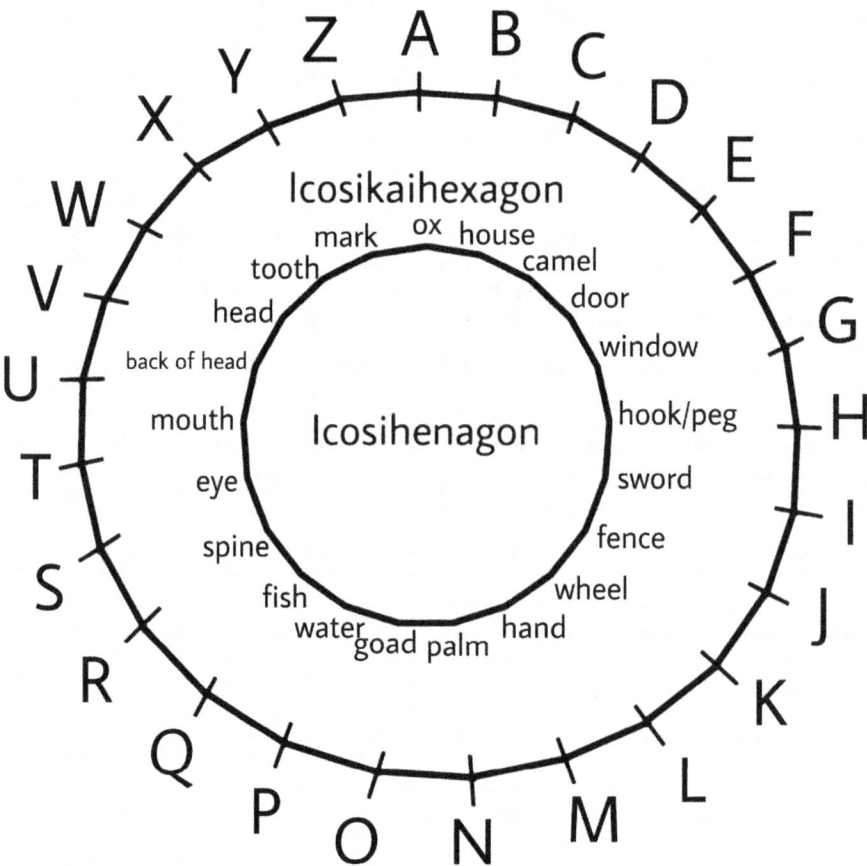

(Chart 2: Phoenician Graphemes to English Graphemes)

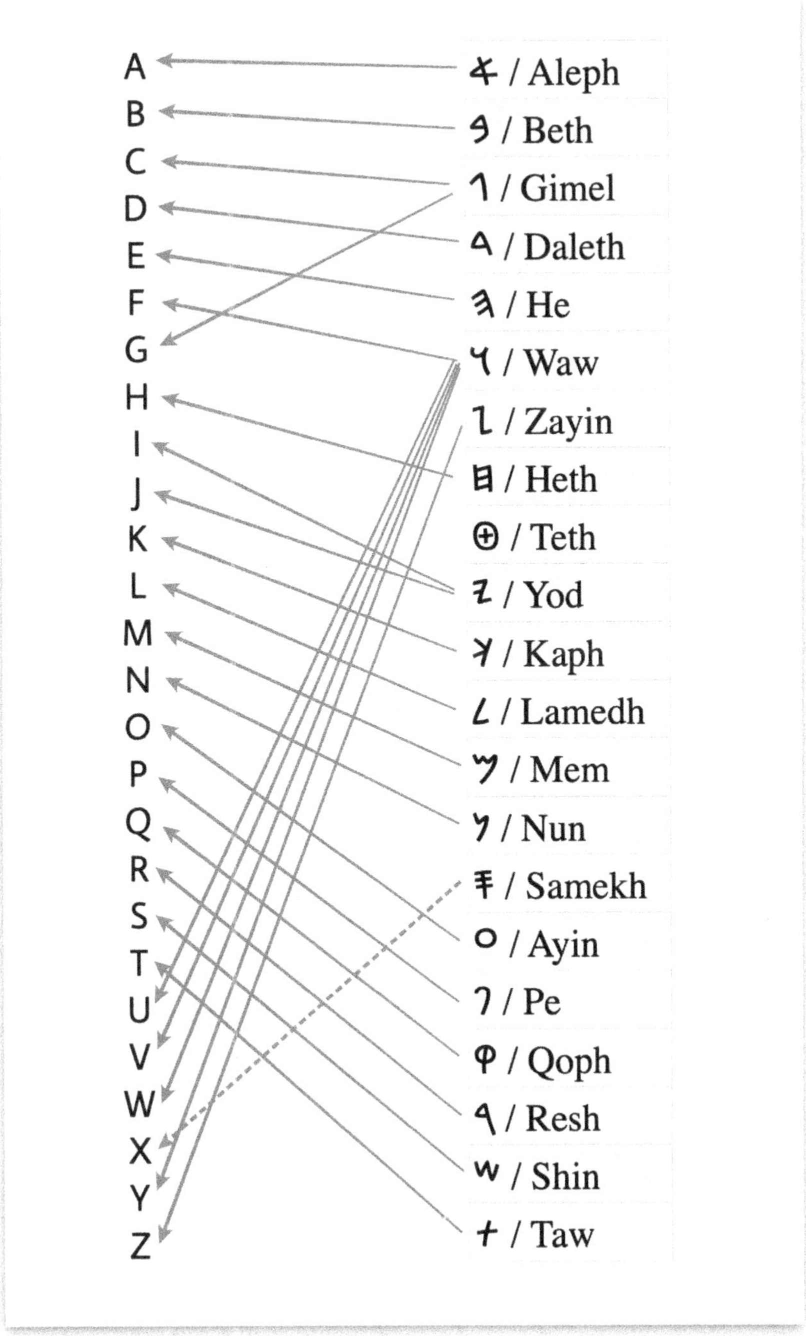
A
B
C
D
E
F
G
H
I
J
K
L
M
N
O
P
Q
R
S
T
U
V
W
X
Y
Z
𐤀 / Aleph
𐤁 / Beth
𐤂 / Gimel
𐤃 / Daleth
𐤄 / He
𐤅 / Waw
𐤆 / Zayin
𐤇 / Heth
𐤈 / Teth
𐤉 / Yod
𐤊 / Kaph
𐤋 / Lamedh
𐤌 / Mem
𐤍 / Nun
𐤎 / Samekh
𐤏 / Ayin
𐤐 / Pe
𐤒 / Qoph
𐤓 / Resh
𐤔 / Shin
𐤕 / Taw

Appendix C: Esoteric and Historical Reference Works

Following is a curated table of **key resources** on runes, Kabbalah, hieroglyphics, and comparative script histories – plus recommended readings for advanced conlang enthusiasts. These works offer deeper dives into the subjects we've touched on, from philological analysis to mystical traditions and practical conlang creation. Each entry includes title, author, date, and a brief summary or note on its relevance:

Icosikaihexagon and Icosihenagon

Reference	Author/Editor	Date	Focus / Summary
Runic and Heroic Poems of the Old Teutonic Peoples	Bruce Dickins	2002 (orig. 1915)	A classic edition of runic poems, exploring the symbolic and magical dimensions of early Germanic staves. Good for historical-linguistic insight.
Prolonged Echoes: Old Norse Myths in Medieval Northern Society	Margaret Clunies Ross	1998	Examines runic usage and mythic contexts. Useful for understanding the synergy of script, religion, and culture in Nordic traditions.
On the Kabbalah and Its Symbolism	Gershom Scholem	1969	Seminal exploration of Hebrew mysticism. Offers insight into how letters function as conduits for divine energies, relevant to ontic alphabets.
Middle Egyptian	James P. Allen	2014	Introduction to Egyptian hieroglyphs, grammar, and culture. Highlights how pictorial references tie into religious practice and cosmic order.
Visible Speech: The Diverse Oneness of Writing Systems	John DeFrancis	1989	Investigates how different scripts reflect cultural realities. Good for comparing the "ontic" impetus across global writing traditions.
The World's Writing Systems	Peter T. Daniels & William Bright (Eds.)	1996	Comprehensive anthology on writing systems worldwide – ranging from alphabets to syllabaries and logographies, with detailed historical context.
A Survey of English Spelling	Edward Carney	1994	Detailed coverage of English orthographic irregularities, bridging them to older genealogies. Good for understanding expansions and merges.
The Art of Language Invention	David J. Peterson	2015	Modern conlang guide by a professional language creator. Offers tips on designing scripts with cultural or symbolic references.
A Secret Vice	J.R.R. Tolkien (ed. with commentary)	Orig. 1930s, published variously	Tolkien's exploration of conlanging. Not purely about alphabets, but essential for seeing how mythic worldbuilding integrates script design.
The Language Construction Kit	Mark Rosenfelder	Ongoing	Renowned online resource (and print versions) guiding conlang creation. Some chapters address script design, symbolic references, and culture.

A Case for Ontolophemes

This **Appendix C** helps direct further study, whether one seeks a deeper philological approach (Daniels & Bright), an esoteric lens (Scholem, Kabbalah), or practical conlang insights (Peterson, Rosenfelder). Each reference illuminates different facets of how scripts arise, evolve, and can be creatively reimagined.

Icosikaihexagon and Icosihenagon

REFERENCES

Allen, J. P. (2014). Middle Egyptian: An introduction to the language and culture of hieroglyphs. Cambridge University Press.

Black, J. A., George, A. R., & Postgate, J. N. (2006). A concise dictionary of Akkadian. Harrassowitz.

Bonfante, L. (1990). Etruscan. University of California Press.

Bosworth, J., & Toller, T. N. (1898). An Anglo-Saxon dictionary. Oxford University Press.

Bottéro, J. (2001). Religion in ancient Mesopotamia. University of Chicago Press.

Carney, E. (1994). A survey of English spelling. Routledge.

Chomsky, N., & Halle, M. (1968). The sound pattern of English. Harper & Row.

Clifford, J. (1986). Writing culture: The poetics and politics of ethnography. University of California Press.

Clunies Ross, M. (1998). Prolonged echoes: Old Norse myths in medieval Northern society. Odense University Press.

Cooper, J. S. (1996). Sumerian and Akkadian in Mesopotamia. In P. T. Daniels & W. Bright (Eds.), The world's writing systems (pp. 37–72). Oxford University Press.

Coulmas, F. (2003). Writing systems: An introduction to their linguistic analysis. Cambridge University Press.

Cross, F. M. (1980). New directions in the study of ancient alphabets. Bulletin of the American Schools of Oriental Research, 238, 1–17.

Crystal, D. (2003). English as a global language (2nd ed.). Cambridge University Press.

Daniels, P. T., & Bright, W. (Eds.). (1996). The world's writing systems. Oxford University Press.

DeFrancis, J. (1984). The Chinese language: Fact and fantasy. University of Hawaii Press.

DeFrancis, J. (1989). Visible speech: The diverse oneness of writing systems. University of Hawaii Press.

Dickins, B. (2002). Runic and heroic poems of the old Teutonic peoples. Boydell & Brewer.

Gelb, I. J. (1952). A study of writing. University of Chicago Press.

Grafton, A., & Most, G. W. (2003). Canon and libraries in the ancient world. Franz Steiner Verlag.

Haarmann, H. (1990). Universal characteristics of symbol systems: Evidence from pictographic scripts. In Signs of civilization (pp. 53–76). Walter de Gruyter.

Halevi, Z. B. (1987). Kabbalah: Tradition of hidden knowledge. Thames and Hudson.

Hsia, A. (1992). Reading Chinese script. Routledge.

Idel, M. (1988). Kabbalah: New perspectives. Yale University Press.

Jeffery, L. H. (1961). The local scripts of archaic Greece. Clarendon Press.

Justeson, J. S., & Stephens, G. D. (1994). The emergence of writing. In Writing in the Maya world (pp. 7–18). University of Pennsylvania Press.

Kaplan, A. (1997). Sefer Yetzirah: The book of creation in theory and practice. Weiser Books.

A Case for Ontolophemes

Kohn, L. (2000). Daoism handbook. Brill.

Kramer, S. N. (1963). The Sumerians: Their history, culture, and character. University of Chicago Press.

Lawlor, R. (1982). Sacred geometry: Philosophy and practice. Thames & Hudson.

Manley, B. (2012). The Penguin historical atlas of Ancient Egypt. Penguin Books.

Page, R. I. (1999). An introduction to English runes (2nd ed.). Boydell Press.

Peterson, D. J. (2015). The art of language invention. Penguin Books.

Postgate, J. N. (1994). Early Mesopotamia: Society and economy at the dawn of history. Routledge.

Sagdeev, A. (1989). Magical aspects of old Turkic inscriptions. Altaica, 12, 20–35.

Sampson, G. (1985). Writing systems: A linguistic introduction. Stanford University Press.

Sass, B. (1988). The genesis of the alphabet and its development in the second millennium B.C. Universitätsverlag Freiburg Schweiz.

Saussure, F. de. (1974). Course in general linguistics (W. Baskin, Trans.). Fontana/Collins. (Original work published 1916)

Scholem, G. (1969). On the Kabbalah and its symbolism. Schocken Books.

Scragg, D. G. (1974). A history of English spelling. Manchester University Press.

Sennrich, R., Haddow, B., & Birch, A. (2016). Neural machine translation of rare words with subword units. In Proceedings of the 54th Annual Meeting of the Association for Computational Linguistics (Vol. 1, pp. 1715–1725).

Smith, B. (2003). Ontology. In L. Floridi (Ed.), Blackwell guide to the philosophy of computing and information (pp. 155–166). Blackwell.

Smith, M. S. (2004). The origins of monotheism in the Bible. Theological Studies Quarterly, 65(2), 1–28.

Wells, J. C. (1982). Accents of English. Cambridge University Press.

Zakaluk, B. L., & Samuels, S. J. (1988). Readability: The limitations of source-based approaches. In S. J. Samuels & M. L. Kamil (Eds.), Reading research: Advances in theory and practice (Vol. 2, pp. 144–179). Academic Press.

Icosikaihexagon and Icosihenagon

To access additional works by Daniel Dinkelman and others, please see the Mythological Center website at www.mythological.center

or scan this QR code:

Copyright 2025 Cineris Multifacet
ISBN: 979-8-89760-036-6

www.ingramcontent.com/pod-product-compliance
Lightning Source LLC
Chambersburg PA
CBHW081151290426
44108CB00018B/2516